A Principle and a Promise

Written by Sharon Sanders

A Principle and a Promise
Trilogy Christian Publishers A Wholly Owned Subsidiary of Trinity Broadcasting Network
2442 Michelle Drive Tustin, CA 92780

Rights Department, 2442 Michelle Drive, Tustin, CA 92780.
Trilogy Christian Publishing/TBN and colophon are trademarks of Trinity Broadcasting Network.
For information about special discounts for bulk purchases, please contact Trilogy Christian Publishing.
Trilogy Disclaimer: The views and content expressed in this book are those of the author and may not necessarily reflect the views and doctrine of Trilogy Christian Publishing or the Trinity Broadcasting Network.
Manufactured in the United States of America
10 9 8 7 6 5 4 3 2 1
Library of Congress Cataloging-in-Publication Data is available.
ISBN: 978-1-63769-322-3
E-ISBN: 978-1-63769-323-0

Dedication

I dedicate *A Principle and a Promise* to the God of Israel, who gave me not only this title but also the final push to complete the writing for "such a time as this" (Esther 4:14). There is nothing more that I desire than He be exalted and honored in His desire is to see mankind follow His path of blessing in Genesis 12:3. As a believer in Jesus, it is my hope that the stand I have taken in this book will be a witness to my Jewish brothers and sisters to let them know that many Christians, like me, follow the God of Israel. If we obey God and watch the principle carry out its mission to bless all who follow His commands in the Genesis factor, we will truly see progress made in Jewish–Christian relations.

Sharon Sanders

Acknowledgments

Eleanor Roosevelt once said, "Many people walk in and out of your life, but only true friends will leave footprints in your heart." My heart is still amazed at the thoughtfulness, encouragement, and faith, which special friends in the Lord have had in me in the writing of this book. There are many who have encouraged me over the years to write, but four special people stand out in my memory. First, I want to salute Marita Brokenshaw, our senior graphic artist for over twenty-five years. Her loyalty to the ongoing ministry in Israel stands out as exceptional. I also wish to thank one of my best friends in this world, Beryl Hunter of the UK. Her continual encouragement and covering me with a lot of prayer through personal intercessors boosted me in strength. Julia Soakell of Christian Friends of Israel UK also helped to organize private prayer warriors who helped to pray me through many obstacles on the road to victory. Then, there is an exceptional friend, the vehicle God used to help launch this book, Tommie Coleman, cofounder with her husband, Robbie, of Zion's Bridge in the United States, who gave me a jump start by pushing me forward to finish and kept energizing me with her intense confidence in my writing. I am eternally grateful. Without these special people and many others who have asked me to write, I could not have accomplished anything. Most of all, thank God for their eternal friendship and love, which I will always cherish.

Sharon Sanders

Endorsements

Sharon Sanders has lived out the name of the ministry she and her husband Ray have led in Jerusalem for over thirty years: "Christian Friends of Israel." Sharon has great gifting as a Bible teacher, but she also models sacrificial love to the people of Israel. *A Principle and a Promise* makes clear why the Genesis 12:3 foundational promise of blessing to those who bless Abraham and his descendants was lost by most of the church through the ages and how its restoration is central to the blessing of individuals, families, churches, and nations. This book is not only a great read but also a good road map for a blessed and fruitful life.

—Rev. Rick Ridings,
Cofounder of Succat Hallel,
24/7 house of worship and prayer in Jerusalem
overlooking the Temple Mount,
International speaker and author,
Chairman of the Board Christian Friends of Israel

At a time when antisemitism and replacement theology are spreading globally, Sharon Sanders's *A Principle and a Promise* is a biblical antidote to those malign influences inside the church. It's a clarion call to walk in the light of God's promises to His chosen people and those who choose to stand with them "for such a time as this."

—Chris Mitchell,
CBN News Middle East bureau chief

Table of Contents

Preface

Christianity is a religion based upon the person and teachings of Jesus of Nazareth. However, Jesus never founded Christianity. He was and is a Jew. He was identified forever to be King of the Jews on His cross—not King of the Christians.

May every believer in Jesus realize that without an understanding of *the Living Torah* (wrongly labeled as the Old Testament), the only Bible from which Jesus taught, they can never come into true fullness and maturity of their faith, as they cannot truly understand the words of Jesus.

Whether you are Protestant, Catholic, or Orthodox, I hope you will see the "pattern" in this book that is woven throughout Scripture, examples of gentiles who touched Jewish lives in a personal way and were greatly blessed. A model blueprint verifies the missing link in today's Christianity. I hope it will enrich your life and help you discover some well-kept secrets.

It's an enlightening journey that begins in Genesis 12:3 and forecasts the final outcome of individuals and nations in relation to its offer. My study is by no means finished but only a beginning of understanding, but I hope it is a start and enough to get you running with the ground rules from God's Word. Do not change lanes halfway through the book. See the race for the discovery of truth all the way to its end. It is my prayer that at the finish line, God will be able to say, "Well done," as stated in Matthew 25:21. I believe the principle we are about to examine was always God's will for us to grasp from the beginning. It's quite sad that it has not been recognized and applied in great ways until now.

This book speaks of the shameful historical atrocities, which Christianity committed against the Jewish people. Much was done in ignorance and by unacceptable teaching about the chosen people. Everyone needs to understand the depth of what took place over a span of two thousand years. Covering it up or complaining, "I'm tired of hearing about it," will not erase the stains of sin on Christendom's garments toward the Jewish people. Two of the greatest transgressions of the church today are Christian antisemitism and replacement theology. Cast them aside and run from everything that will hinder you from winning the prize which Jesus is waiting to give at the end of your life...find the path of blessing through obedience.

The blessing does not require anyone to become "legalistic." It does not ask for any gentile to "convert" to Judaism. It simply commands Christians to be in the right relationship with Israel. According to God's Word and the expectation of those who have been granted mercy through the Lord Jesus, this is our duty: to seek the welfare of Israel.

Many treasures of the Torah, Shabbat, and God's feasts, which Jesus celebrated, as well as His Jewishness, were lost through centuries of theological error. Herewith, I have introduced the visual correlation of church graveyards because it seems appropriate to uncover the evidence of the church's abandonment of the Jews. The church simply buried the essential precondition to find the road of blessing for mankind and forfeited, to a great extent, the benevolence of God.

Sadly, today Judaism and Christianity are two separate faith communities torn from one another by centuries of misunderstandings. Jesus never taught against His people. He was devoted to and still loves His Jewish family from which He came, but all indications are that much of Christianity has a spiritual problem, laying within its bosom. Christian antisemitism is the knife stuck within its heart, believing He threw up His hands and abandoned them. So, let's not be ignorant. Once someone comes into the understanding of Israel's God-given role to the nations, they are closer to healing and wholeness.

Some church members have been born in Christian homes, while others joined a traditional denomination later in life. Many followers of Jesus have come out of cathedrals, abbeys, megachurches, and traditional houses of worship but are not aligned with any particular denomination today. Some awoke to spirit-filled or independent fellowships. Those who follow "The Way" (followers of Yeshua) need to realize that there was a time when much of the church got off track and forfeited God's cup of blessing through the centuries. They wandered off the path God had set before them and ended up in a field of betrayal and treason toward Israel.

What about those who say that they believe in replacement theology, the doctrine that the church has replaced Israel and the Jewish people? The Bible has warned against putting the Jewish people asunder (Isaiah 56:3). It is something essentially akin to receiving the most beautiful gift from the Jewish people you could ever imagine and then walking away with the gift, never even saying thank you for giving all we possess spiritually. I must speak about the shame that Christianity brought upon itself because of the unbelievable legacy of hatred left behind in preceding centuries.

Christianity's halls of learning did not teach the language of Jesus (Hebrew or Aramaic), nor the restoration appointed for Israel. Most sermons never touch on Romans, chapters nine, ten, and eleven, passages that are imperative for every believer in Jesus to understand the requirements in relation to the Jewish people. Preordination classroom education has rarely considered these keys to blessing.

Romans 11:22 is clear that those who have come into the kingdom, which the Master taught on continually, need to treat the Jewish people the same way in which they themselves, as gentiles, have been treated (through the mercy of God) or they will be cut off. This warning has yet to be put into a teaching tool on the internet for a worldwide audience. And yet, the Bible gives this warning twice.

> For if God spared not the natural branches, take heed lest He also spare not thee. Behold therefore the goodness and severity of God: on them which fell, severity; but toward thee, goodness, if thou continue

in His goodness: (toward the Jewish people) otherwise, thou also shalt be cut off.

Romans 11:21-22 (KJV)

Korah, in Numbers, chapter sixteen, spread a spirit of dissent and rebellion among his fellow congregational members, blaming Moses and Aaron as he drew his friends into his way of thinking. God does not author church splits but instead desires unity for His name's sake. Israel needs to be a unifying cord connecting us, not tearing us apart.

When discerning anti-Israel churches, we should be careful not to judge severely, for only God sees the heart of man. Let us not fall into the trap of a divisive critical spirit in regard to Israel and the Genesis 12:3 principle and its promise.

We need to do all we can to promote unity in the Spirit, as long as we are not embracing that which is against God. God has not given any of us the authority to condemn or judge our brothers and sisters, in or out of the church, but sometimes we have to agree to disagree. I do not want to place the blame of Christian antisemitism on any Christian leader, for there were, and still are, many antisemites. But, when history teaches reality, all followers of Jesus must accept responsibility for the mistakes the church forefathers made and share the unpleasant, but nonetheless, the whole truth about the deception many live under today.

Respectfully, let us be slow to write off everyone in the church because they do not have a heart for Israel or understand the meaning of Genesis 12:3. Most importantly, I am asking everyone who reads this book, if you see its truths, not to criticize your pastor or spiritual leader if they cannot see the place of Israel in the faith.

This book is meant to bring a blessing, and if you see it, rejoice in the Lord and share it. If you present this book to your pastor, and he still doesn't see the key to blessing, then rejoice that you were able to share with him, but still love him and continue to pray for him. If he is teaching against Israel, this requires serious prayer. In belonging to a church or congregation, we are still subject to the elders (1 Peter 5:5). Be careful to pray for your spiritual leaders, in the Lord's love, and grant them space to come into the understanding of Israel, in His timing. The best action one can then initiate is to pray for them out of love and wait for God to open up their hearts.

In the meantime, enjoy the book and, whatever you learn, know that it is based upon absolute truth! For some, it may be a hard pill to swallow; but as difficult as it may be to accept what took place with the pointing of the finger at the Jewish people in the name of Jesus, the most detrimental separation that ever happened in the spiritual world must be acknowledged by Christians.

I hope this book will help Christian leaders realize that they have been "robbed" of spiritual knowledge and understanding about our Jewish heritage. May many come to realize the missing link (Israel) in their faith and seek to play a part in the repair work that needs to be done in relationships with the Jewish people.

Introduction

The Bible teaches that we are to bless and support the Jewish people and the nation of Israel. It warns against bringing harm to either land or people (Psalm 83; Zechariah 1:15). To not seek Israel's welfare is something like receiving the most beautiful gift you've ever had from them, saying, "Thanks," taking the gift from them, and walking away. It is like a slap in the face. The Jewish people gave the Christian church everything we spiritually possess.

In the early days, Jewish believers in Jesus worshipped with God's chosen people in Jewish places of worship. The separation from Judaism that eventually took place ripped into pieces the tolerance they shared. Sadly, today Judaism and Christianity are two distinctly different faith communities severed from one another by centuries of deep-seated hatred and misunderstandings.

Jesus never taught against His People. He loved and still loves His Jewish family from which He came. Still, all indications are that much of Christianity has a spiritual problem laying within its bosom, Christian antisemitism, the knife stuck within it.

As Christians are grafted-in citizens of Israel's Commonwealth through the Messiah, Jesus (Romans 11:17), it is my prayer that spiritual fullness and maturity will bring everyone into a deeper relationship with God.

Everyone needs to know the importance of the Genesis 12:3 principle with its origin and foundation rooted in God's heart. The Bible clearly teaches that anyone who blesses the Jewish people will be blessed.

Perhaps you have had concerns about whether you should support the Jewish people but are not sure how to provide support. It is for that purpose this book has been written. I trust it will enlighten your path to guide you in your desire to align with Genesis 12:3. The principle and the promise will introduce ways in which you can be a blessing to Israel: prayer, practical action, financial support, as well as being a reconciler, a true witness, and a holy light and standing for truth.

No matter how sincere you might be or how hard you try, unless you have the right key, you cannot open a locked door. The Bible is the tool that unlocks the door to understanding the Jewish people. Each example I've chosen from the Word of God concerning gentiles who blessed the Jewish people brought a sweet-smelling savor to God as they carried out His will in following the principle and the promise of Genesis 12:3.

While compiling this small book, I encountered a powerful, spiritual struggle for time in the race to get to the finish line. I felt all along that something or someone was trying to prevent me from completing this writing. However, I also recognized that God pushed me onward to cross over the finish line and meet my goal. My story of the principle is by no means complete, but I believe this book is in the right timing of God, and He gave me the perseverance I needed to finish.

My intentions are not to present a formula for high-speed material gain. It is written with sincere hope for those who have a heartfelt desire to be a blessing to Israel and who might come into a righteous relationship with the chosen people of Israel. By being open-minded, those who embrace the Genesis 12:3 principle would be rewarded for having the same desire as God's heart.

Once again, Romans 11:22 is clear that those who have come into the kingdom, which the Master taught on continually, needed to treat the Jewish people the same way they have been treated (through the mercy of God), or they would be cut off. Little attention has been given to this portion of Scripture, and yet, the Bible gives a warning twice. "Therefore consider the goodness and severity of God: on those who fell, severity; but toward you, goodness, if you continue in His goodness. Otherwise you also will be cut off" (Romans 11:22).

It's my prayer that you will continue reading with expectancy. In the words of a good friend,

> While I never deliberately contemplated plagiarizing and did all I could to avoid the same—it remains possible, when following tradition, to have modestly crossed the line at some unknown point. This seems nearly inevitable to me because I readily sought and generously used many good written and oral sources

during my research for the verbal presentation stage. All of my known sources are accurately cited.[1]

The books I've read and studied through the years, especially the Bible, the teachings I've attentively listened to and absorbed, have become part of who I am, and therefore, are poured out onto these pages. The Holy Spirit helped me recall the richness of my studies that I share in this book. This I know: once someone understands Israel's God-given role to the nations, Jews and Christians will be closer to wholeness and healing in their relationships.

An Ancient and Everlasting Promise

All Scripture is given by inspiration of God, and is profitable for doctrine, for reproof, for correction, for instruction in righteousness.

2 Timothy 3:16

As a Christian leader living in Israel since 1985, I continued studying the Jewish Scriptures (Torah) in my hunger for spiritual nourishment. As I searched for deeper meaning, I believe I heard God's voice behind the words speaking to my heart and saying, "Do you see the pattern?" Once I saw it, I knew I had discovered an intriguing treasure. It was there all the time but had been buried in the sands of time and disconnect. As I continued my insatiable desire to learn more, I became increasingly captivated with each new unearthing carefully shadowed but overlapped in a number of passages parallel in meaning. My hunch was finally confirmed when I realized that I had happened upon a Divine precept—a desire of the Almighty that would bring subsequent blessings to all who followed His commands. I knew I could not dismiss this clear and genuine desire of God's heart.

It is truly a divine pattern woven in Scripture resembling the love of God for His chosen people, artistically and beautifully interlaced throughout the Bible like a mysterious love note He wants us to find. I wanted to shout my little discovery from the highest mountain for all the world to hear. Unfortunately,

Sunday school lessons based upon the fundamental principle of blessing the Jewish people are in short supply in Christianity's arena of Christian education, so I thought I had to share what I had found.

The treasure of blessing in the pattern I had discovered was the exact result of following Genesis 12:3. Its power drew me like a magnet to undertake an exciting, intensive search for more of the design God had woven throughout His Word. What transpired warmed my heart as I felt that I had stumbled upon a neglected major principle of blessing Israel. I thought this inspiration could be a real blessing to so many who have received so much from the Jewish people. The principle itself had always been intermingled throughout the writings but had fallen between the cracks of history from the human eye; therefore, veiled to the average reader. Because Genesis 12:3 rarely was taught from Christian pulpits by men and women of the cloth, its importance has been mostly overlooked. A shrouded perception of the church and their responsibility to God's chosen people had more or less been forgotten and sometimes forbidden by the church hierarchy.

While my husband and I had been practicing the principle of "I will bless those who bless you, And I will curse him who curses you; And in you all the families of the earth shall be blessed" (Genesis 12:3), actually finding the underlying law of reciprocity and how to carry it out in various individual lives really brought the biblical promise to the forefront in my own understanding.

I am convinced that the Lord organized the Genesis 12:3 promise to be written down near the beginning of His Word as a guide to the source of His desire to bless humanity, which proves His love for all mankind. It spoke to me clearly that there was an eagerness in God's heart to bless His creation, and He made the blessing known at the start. All one has had to do is engage the principle. I am left with no other explanation: God yearns to invoke a blessing upon those who desire to receive it. When gentiles grasp the principle, they touch a special place in His heart.

Today, enlightened Christians and friends of Israel around the world often use Genesis 12:3 as the basis for their work on behalf of the Jewish nation. However, because of two thousand years of church neglect of the Jewish Scriptures, the principle was never taken too seriously. Someone once said that "it is as if God threw away a teacup because He was finished with the tea." This has been the attitude of the church toward the "Old" Testament and its promises to the patriarchs for way too long.

God truly was with the children of Israel as they bore witness of God's presence in the ancient world. I believe loving the Jewish people is perhaps one of King David's "keys" to God's eternal kingdom, considering that over each of the twelve gates, the name of one of the twelve tribes of Israel is engraved (Revelation 21:12). This shows the importance of His chosen people to God. How is it going to be possible for anyone who hates Israel to walk through a gate of salvation? That may come as a real surprise to Christians, but it's in the Bible. "Also she had a great and high wall with twelve gates, and twelve angels at the gates, and names written on them, which are the names of the twelve tribes of the children of Israel" (Revelation 21:12).

Once acted upon, Genesis 12:3 becomes a sweet-smelling savor to God because we are pleasing God by obeying this principle. We lay up "treasures in heaven," eternal blessings that moths cannot destroy, and thieves cannot break in and steal (Matthew 6:19). The principle was meant to be taken seriously and never meant to be grasped lightly as if not on God's priority list. One clearly can see that avoiding or ignoring His offer has and will continue to affect Christendom and all nations. Through personal reflection and prayer, Christian clergy and other church leaders need to take heed and be wise to pause and consider God's offer.

God never changes. His everlasting Word remains in place from generation to generation. If you are a Christian or not and feel no interest in God's offer of blessing, that is your choice. However, perhaps you are a spiritual leader and are not interested in God's proposal; in that case, you may fail to fully prepare your flock for the days ahead, especially at the judgment of the "sheep and goats" upon the Lord's glorious return and coming (Matthew 25:31-46).

For a genuine revival, restoration, and longed-for reformation to occur in Christian churches, acknowledgment and repentance for the wrong that has been done to the Jewish people by the church are required by God's justice and holiness.

Various biblical sources throughout history have recorded monumental miracles that God performed for the Hebrew children. When He brought them out of Egypt and through the Red Sea by His mighty arm, those exciting and forever unforgettable events reverberated at full volume throughout the ancient world. They have remained the media buzz for time immemorial.

Ancient cultures and idol worshippers involved in the trade of goods and services would have come into contact with Hebrews who followed the Torah (books of Moses). Even through the ancient Mediterranean grapevine, news spread rapidly of what the God of Israel had done for the Hebrews. Still, many gentiles hardened their hearts and became Israel's enemy—even today.

So it was with the pharaoh, who had begun to view the Hebrews as a threat. He said to his people,

> Look, the people of Israel are more and mightier than we; come, let us deal shrewdly with them, lest they multiply, and it happen, in the event of war, that they also join our enemies and fight against us, and so go up out of the land.
>
> Exodus 1:9-10

He placed the Hebrew children into bondage for many years until Moses was raised up by God to deliver them from his cruelty.

The pharaoh obviously was a proud leader who praised himself by proclaiming, "I am in control," but God had the last word.

It has been said that the pharaoh's illusion was a dominating God-type of supremacy that made the pharaoh all the more defenseless against the power of almighty God. This point should be remembered as we visualize, in the next chapters, each individual who, throughout history, stood facing a Jewish person or a community of Jewish people in need and had to make a decision. On the one hand, we see gentiles excelling in making good personal choices and acting honorably. On the other hand, we see many failing miserably in their God-given opportunities to receive blessings from God.

Those who have cursed Israel down through the ages have made poor decisions and displayed the weakness of their character. God, who watches over the nations and observes all actions, especially toward His chosen people, brought severe consequences upon Egypt for cursing the Jews when they fled their bondage, "You showed signs and wonders against Pharaoh, Against all his servants, And against all the people of his land. For You knew that they acted proudly against them" (Nehemiah 9:10).

When the Jews were in exile under the leadership of Nehemiah, the Levites read to them from the Books of Moses (Torah) about an event that occurred during the exodus from Egypt: "No Ammonite or Moabite should ever come into the assembly of God because they had not met the children of Israel with bread and water, but hired Balaam against them to curse them" (Nehemiah 13:1-2).

The Ammonites and Moabites paid a considerable price for their arrogance toward the Jews. God yearns to bless those who desire to obey His commands. When non-Jews grasp the Genesis 12:3 principle, they touch a special place in His heart. We see this happening today among new Iranian believers in Jesus: once entering the faith, they are given a heart of love for Israel. It is amazing. We personally encountered this phenomenon when in Kuala Lumpur, the capital of Indonesia.

I want to stress that the Torah is, without a doubt, a love story between the God of the universe and His chosen people. As Christians, we need to be mindful that Jesus (Yeshua, in Hebrew) was an Orthodox Jewish rabbi in the flesh. He taught His disciples from the scrolls of the Hebrew Scriptures, which was the primary source of all of His teaching. If it were not for the Jewish Scriptures, the New Testament would make no sense to us as Jesus fulfilled the Jewish Scriptures, and He taught them every day of His life. Among all the books written about the miracles Jesus performed while on earth, books that were too many to list (John 20:30-31), it is entirely possible that He might have taught on Genesis 12:3 when He opened the scroll to *Bereshit* (Genesis) in the synagogue.

Because of neglect of the Jewish Scriptures, much of the church forfeited centuries of spiritual blessings. Many assumed that they just didn't need the "old" portion of the Bible because the "new" had replaced the old (so they thought). It may be long overdue, but never too late to say that historical church leaders made a tragic mistake and led many of their flocks astray when it came to the chosen people. The leaven of a wrong doctrine was not new to Jesus. There was errant doctrine during His time on earth as well.

Every Christian must come to the realization that there was no religion nor institution called Christianity during the lifetime of Jesus. His disciples continued to meet in the temple even after Jesus' resurrection. They took the first step in being called "Christians" at Antioch (Acts 11:26). Antioch was an ancient city located on the Orontes River near the Amanus Mountains in Syria. His disciples were known as "Nazarenes." The Jewish lawyer, Tertullus, records that "the Jews call us Nazarenes." While around AD 331, Eusebius records that Christ was called a Nazorean (used in the Greek New Testament) from the town of Nazareth.[2] *Notzrim* is the modern Hebrew word for Christians.

In its infancy, seeds of false doctrines were sown like tares among the wheat by church leaders as early as the late first century. The effect of those flawed and rotten seeds is still bearing bad fruit prevalent in many of today's churches. Bumper crops have grown in the name of "replacement theology" in the pastures of many shepherds of Christianity.

Many Christians hold to the teaching that the Jewish people have failed in their mission for God because they rejected Jesus, and that God is finished with them forever, and that they have subsequently abrogated their right to be a "light to the nations" (Isaiah 49:6). Just a little scholarly training in this type of Christian education would reveal that this is not true.

Historical records tell us that an angry mob of religious leaders in Israel cried out, "Crucify Him." It definitely was not the entire nation.[3] A recent archaeological excavation gives considerable evidence that Jesus was condemned in the courtyard of Herod's complex, which would have been able to hold only around one hundred people.[4] This archaeological evidence may challenge our traditions and expose evidence for truth.

There were multitudes from every walk of life who loved Jesus and followed Him everywhere to hear His teachings and encounter His miracles. The New Testament has countless accounts confirming this awareness. Furthermore, I also understand that "all have sinned, and fall short of the glory of God" (Romans 3:23). God will once again show mercy to Israel. On His cross, He forgave them (Luke 23:34). After His death, Peter preached to about three thousand Jews who asked forgiveness for missing the mark with Jesus. (Acts 2:36-40). From my point of view, what would have happened had Jesus not died for the sins of Israel and all of mankind? Nothing was a surprise to the Father who had sent His Son to die.

Paul (his real name is Shaul) and his words have been misrepresented many times, so we must carefully read his epistles to understand the church's connection to Israel. Such as this verse:

For if you were cut out of the olive tree which is wild by nature, and were grafted contrary to nature into a cultivated olive tree, how much more will these, who are natural branches, be grafted into their own olive tree?

Romans 11:24

Notice that the Jews to whom Paul refers are called "natural branches" to be grafted back into their own olive tree.

God's forgiving heart is something we cannot totally comprehend in its fullness. I know that His eternal covenant and promises for the Jewish people are for all time. We must make a serious effort to uproot the heresy of replacement theology, also known as "supersessionism" or "dominion theology," which has been sown in place of the truth of His unchanging covenant with Israel. Replacement theology has become the most dangerous doctrine in the church today. Why would I make such a statement? Because nations will be judged according to how they treated Israel when Jesus returns.[5]

I believe another key to the coming kingdom overlooked in today's churches is the revelatory truth that redeemed gentiles through Jesus have been grafted in as citizens of the Commonwealth of Israel: "that at that time you were without Christ, being aliens from the commonwealth of Israel and strangers from the covenants of promise, having no hope and without God in the world" (Ephesians 2:12).

Because of Christ's tearing down of the middle wall of partition that kept us away from worshipping in the temple, we are ushered in through God's mercy. (Ephesians 2:14). We are brought in by His mercy. Christ did not divorce Israel and swap wives in order for non-Jews to take the place of His beloved Israel, the "apple of His Eye."[6] Followers of Jesus are included; they are incorporated and joined to the Commonwealth of a redeemed Israel, which will arise in the future upon His return.

> Now, therefore, you are no longer strangers and foreigners, but fellow citizens with the saints and members of the household of God, having been built on the foundation of the apostles and prophets, Jesus Christ Himself being the chief cornerstone.
>
> Ephesians 2:19-20

We must awaken to the realization that in the final stage of the establishment of God's kingdom, there will be no one found believing a lie (Revelation 22:15). Antisemitism and replacement theology are lies. If not repentant, anyone practicing these false teachings the Bible says will not be allowed into God's eternal kingdom. "Outside are dogs and sorcerers and sexually immoral and murderers and idolaters, and whoever loves and practices a lie" (Revelation 22:15).

A trend in America during these days of COVID-19 is a downward shift away from traditional denominations. While Americans remain primarily religious, only 30 percent identify with a particular Protestant denomination.[7] I believe that there would be less decline if they would place Israel on their agendas and in their bulletins each Sunday for sincere and loving prayer. Why? Because at least they would be propelling a blessing into the prayer realm and show that they care.

While declining numbers in the church set off alarm bells, perhaps church leaders should ask, "Where is our logjam?" I learned that when professional loggers discover a logjam, one of them climbs a large tree near the river so he can look over the problem and find the cause. What he is looking for is the "key log" creating the jam. Once removed, the river takes care of the rest. An inexperienced person could spend hours, days, or even weeks moving logs around without results. If your church is teaching replacement theology, look no further. Your church has a logjam!

In this history-making and world-changing era, Bible prophecy in Israel is being noted even by non-believers in an attempt to grasp all that is happening. Therefore, Christian leaders need to offer solid food on the Bible menu during church services. Bible prophecy is the meat on the platter needed to prepare for the second coming of Jesus. In many churches, the servings fall short of the biblical nutrients necessary for healthy congregations.

The Word of God taught in context is extremely important in this clarion call to teach about Israel. It will take the meat of the Word to satisfy hungry sheep. Homilies and sermons with no reference to Bible prophecy, the second coming of Christ, and God's plans and purposes for Israel miss the mark of excellence in today's spiritual quest for learning in Christian education.

The hour is late, and Christians need to be praying, with wisdom and understanding, about the signs of the times, as did the men of Issachar (1 Chronicles 12:32), whose tribe was one of the twelve tribes of Israel. What is happening in Israel today is the most significant sign of the Lord's return and is the key to world redemption. Why wouldn't we want our congregations to know the key players at the end of days?

I have encountered troubled pastors and clergy who have made an emotional appeal for help in understanding Israel. Out of frustration and desperation, some said, "Teach us what we missed in seminary and Bible college. We are ready!" One pastor sadly felt the exclusion of not knowing the truth and said, "Why didn't I hear about all of this sooner?" Another Christian brother, with heartache in his soul, said, "I spent twenty-five years in the pulpit, and I've never before heard what I just learned! Why?"

I shall never forget the pastor who said to me, "I have pastored for many years, and until I spent time in Israel and met the Jewish people, I never knew the depth of spiritual understanding the Jewish people possess. I can't begin to hold a candle to their biblical knowledge." It has been said that we cannot pretend to understand what we do not know or have not experienced.

God's servant leaders must staunchly and, without apology, support the truth that there can be no second coming of Jesus without the nation of Israel! Jesus will not return to a Palestinian state, nor will He stand on the Temple Mount with an Islamic flag flying in the wind, reminding Him to bow to Allah, the Muslim god.

The Genesis 12:3 principle and its overall fundamental proposition can be attached to the golden rule of brotherhood: "And just as you want men to do to you, you also do to them likewise" (Matthew 7:12). Keep in mind that Genesis 12:3 was originally given to Abram (whose name was later changed to Abraham) during a time when the church did not yet exist. When God spoke to Abraham of "His people," He meant the Hebrew children, the Israelites. The absolute truth is that God's covenant with Israel has never been abolished, and woe to anyone who tries to work against it.

I believe true blessings follow when God's principle returns to them through spiritual, emotional, physical, and sometimes material benefits, but to adhere to the principle as a formula for gain invokes a wrong motive. Genesis 12:3 suggests that God desired to bless the multitudes through Abraham: "I will bless [all] those who bless you [plural], but him [singular] who speaks lightly of you [*kal*, meaning "light"] I will ensnare." In other words, whoever takes the unconditional Abrahamic covenant lightly will be ensnared and confounded by the LORD God of Israel."[8] The warning within this verse is not to be dismissed.

The "covenant between the parts" (Genesis 15:7-21) that God made with Abraham is neither conditional nor insignificant.[9]

Multitudes of sheep on every continent sit in church pews, waiting to hear more about Israel and its chosen people regarding the role they play in the end times. As my husband and I traveled the world, we spoke to countless churches in over fifty nations. Many believers hold a real interest in Israel but sometimes hesitate to ask a speaker to talk to the congregation about Israel since the church's connection to Israel was not taught before by their pastor. Most pastors in our churches were never educated in Bible colleges and seminaries about Israelology; therefore, they cannot speak on it themselves, which can cause suspicion or insecurity in considering themselves as inadequate in their learning.

Other Christians want to talk about the love in their hearts for the Jewish people at church but are afraid to bring up the subject with their leaders. Pastors need not be threatened by the fact that, in some situations, congregants are more knowledgeable about Israel and the end times than themselves. It is not something that should cause alarm.

Derek Prince concluded lukewarm powerlessness can be attributed to antisemitism and can be remedied through repentance and renunciation.[10] Fortunately, many sheep have experienced the Holy Spirit's move in their lives that included receiving a love for Israel. There is no need for fear or intimidation. God so wants to awaken the Body of Christ worldwide.

The church needs to realize that Jesus will be returning to the same earthly city from which He departed. When He returns, He will establish the Messianic kingdom of one thousand years (Revelation 20:1-8). Later, when New Jerusalem, the Holy City, comes down from heaven to earth, it will still be Jewish in character (Revelation 21:10-14).

Jesus clearly spoke in Matthew, chapter twenty-four, of the physical signs to watch before His return. First, he warned everyone not to fall prey to deception, which would be rampant. He then advised everyone to stay focused on the parable of the fig tree. "When its branch has already become tender; and puts forth leaves, you know that summer is near. So, you also, when you see these things happening, know that it is near—at the doors" (Mark 13:28-29).

His admonition to rulers, leaders, and wise servants who are spiritual overseers is not to be missed. Leaders need to be found when He comes serving meat, not milk (1 Corinthians 3:1-3) to hungry sheep. The era of "feel good" sermons and messages on affluence and prosperity is somewhat unbalanced as there is so much more to teach. The church needs to bring new light and understanding into the lives of our congregants in view of our recent times of the pandemic and quarantines.

I was often puzzled why anyone needed a success message when they could have the Lord's blessings on their lives by obeying the Genesis 12:3 principle. It is a guide to a successful life. The Hebrew word for prosperity is *salach*. It leans toward getting things done and to wholeness of body, soul, and spirit rather than material benefits.

According to *Strong's Exhaustive Concordance of the Bible*, another Hebrew word for prosperity is *shalom*. For Christians, it means the peace that Christ achieved on the cross, a complete and whole peace. Also, *shalom* means completeness, soundness, welfare, and peace. "Give, and it will be given to you" (Luke 6:38). "I will bless those who bless you" (Genesis 12:3). It is extremely important in our walk with the Lord that we have no antisemitism in our hearts. You cannot be antisemitic and have peace in your heart. It is not possible.

Each of us must qualify to be a part of the coming kingdom of God on earth: "That you may be counted worthy of the kingdom of God [...] since it is a righteous thing with God to repay with tribulation those who trouble you" (2 Thessalonians 1:5-6).

In recent years, God has been calling His Jewish people back to Israel, the homeland He established. He stands by His heavenly window, watching as they continue to return. Even during COVID-19, they continue to return. His promises for Israel and His chosen people are remarkable. We are blessed to live and be involved in this epochal time of Israel's re-gathering, restoration, and redemption, the continuous budding of the fig tree.

How exciting it was for me to comprehend God's divine plan for Israel. I have never lost my enthusiasm for sharing with the church the many scriptural promises for Israel. Whenever I speak or teach, I try to serve meat on the menu, feeding as many as I can with prophetical food for today.

As this first chapter comes to a close, my firm and unmovable position is that the keystone of my salvation is Jesus. What He accomplished as the Lamb of God, my substitute sacrifice, can never be reproduced. He is the one who unlocks heaven's gates and gives us a heart connected to His. Wherever this book takes wing in the world, I hope that it will land in the lap of everyone who follows Jesus, so they will understand the Genesis 12:3 principle and know that its accompanying promise of blessings still stands in today's world.

Church, My Christian Heritage

Start children off on the way they should go, and even when they are old they will not turn from it.

Proverbs 22:6 (NIV)

World War II ended not long before I was born, which was on the eve before Rosh HaShanah on the Jewish calendar—New Beginnings. The Depression left its mark on communities across America. Despite the intense struggles so many faced, our farming community continued to work hard at pioneering the prairie lands into golden fields of wheat and grain. Our community believed that hard work resulted in progress.

I spent a lot of time in church activities. I grew up in the Midwest in the Methodist Church in Hartsburg, Illinois (USA), and went to church every Sunday morning. Our charming country church was painted white with black shutters. A large bell on top rang throughout our village when services were about to begin. It was our community meeting place with God.

In the sanctuary were rows of wooden pews, where everyone had their own designated row and seat, as well as an organ, piano, wall clock, and a railing used to kneel for the Lord's Supper or Communion. Engraved on the Communion altar in the center of the sanctuary were the words "In Remembrance of Me." These American furnishings were part of the permanent church fixtures in our traditional place of worship.

As children, we loved to play and recite a little jingle in Sunday school. While locking our hands and twisting them outward, we'd bring our two thumbs together, which made the doors of a church. Then, the first two fingers of the left and right hands went upward, forming a steeple. We then recited a little ditty that went like this: "Here's the church, here's the steeple, open it up and see all the people!"

To show how many weeks we attended Sunday school, little silver stars were pasted onto our attendance cards, not because of intensive learning of the roots of our faith but because we were good children and we had attended Sunday school.

We put a penny into the little lighthouse, which lit up when the penny was inserted. This helped us learn that we were supposed to be a light to all mankind. An old song called "The Lighthouse" reminded us that we were to be the light that shines in the darkness and that it would lead us safely home. Jesus, of course, was the Lighthouse, and we owed our lives to Him.

We went to hear reverend so-and-so preach every Sunday morning and joined the church through membership and passing our confirmation classes. We were "confirmed" in the church through sacraments and religious instruction. I, like the other girls, wore my new white communion dress with matching shoes and received my white, zippered, first Bible.

Our small village was graced with three different denominations: Methodist, Lutheran, and Baptist. Everyone was very friendly toward one another in my hometown, but few had little to do with each other when it came to religious activities or spiritual matters. Each church lived according to their own denominational practices. Of one thing I am certain: in all of our churches, there were no Bible studies held on the Jewishness of Jesus, what nation He belonged to, or anything regarding his manhood telling us who He really was: a Jew.

The church building was overseen by the Methodist Church, the denomination to which we belonged. Much later in life, when I became "born again," I learned that the building on the corner was not the church; it was the people within the building.

We sang about Jesus in Sunday school and were taught, as a congregation, to pray the Lord's Prayer, "Our Father Who Art in Heaven," and often recited the twenty-third psalm in unison. We addressed all our prayers "Dear Father," but I never knew He had identified Himself in the Bible as the God of Abraham, Isaac, and Jacob, or that He was the God of Israel.

When we sang "A Mighty Fortress is our God," I thought he was "our God" only. I never knew He had revealed Himself and made a covenant with other people before the church. He had no name, no identity, and I knew nothing except that He was "God."

We sang "The First Noel" at Christmastime: "Noel, Noel, Noel, Noel, born is the King of Israel." "O Come, O Come, Emmanuel and ransom captive Israel" was another song. The name Israel was sung, but no one asked where Israel was or about who we were singing.

When I was three years old in 1948, the year Israel became a nation, my mother stood me on a chair behind the pastor's pulpit to sing for our congregation. She and my sister helped me memorize the traditional hymn, "Holy, Holy Holy." But it was a long time before I understood the One to whom I sang. Was He God of the Buddhists? God of the Hindus? I don't suppose anyone would have ever said He was "God of the Jews" during those years! I was taught to love God, respect my parents, and read the Bible. But I knew nothing about Him except that He was the "God" of the church.

My father told me that our roots were from the Roman Catholic Church, also known as the universal "mother" church. The Roman Catholic Church was seen as the "mother" church and spoken about in the Apostle's Creed, which we all recited in the congregational meeting each Sunday.

Today the meaning of the word "church" is so different from when I was a child. It now covers a wide scope of interpretations and does not mean the same to everyone.

The Greek word *ecclesia* is translated as "church" and means "a body of unified people." In other words, there is nothing particularly Christian about the term "church" because the Bible tells us that early followers of Jesus also met in homes, beside rivers, on mountain slopes, and in other quiet places. Dr. Eli Lizorkin-Eyzenberg once said that it is simply inaccurate to say "church" instead of the more appropriate word "assembly" or "gathering," but...that is the way we all grew up. We just naturally go to church.[11]

When church bells rang in America, I had no idea that it brought back terrible memories to Jews who had immigrated to the "New World" after the Holocaust. But now, I am sure they remember that their kinsmen passed churches and heard church bells while boarded up in cattle cars on the way to Auschwitz concentration camps. It made a chill go down their backs. I'm sure they remembered how a loved one traveled on those death trains past country churches on the way to their execution.

It was many years after moving to Israel that I learned that some German churches actually "sang louder" when the cattle cars passed by on Sunday mornings, taking Jews to the ovens.[12] "If you say but we knew nothing about this, does not He who weighs the heart perceive it?" (Proverbs 24:12).

No one wanted to talk about the atrocities they had seen while in Sunday school or church services in Europe. At the time, the church hierarchy wrapped their sermons in a blanket of replacement theology, and no one knew what that meant. The Jews just weren't relevant. Christians were taught to look the other way.

I often speak to groups who traditionally believe they are part of the church by having membership in a particular denomination. Others tell me not to consider them part of the church anymore. Still, others write me and say they are part of the bride, the true church. Finally, others want nothing to do with Christendom but believe in Jesus. There are so many diverse opinions.

It took a Jewish immigrant from the former Soviet Union to ask me, "Sharon, what god do the Christians worship?" I was shocked. Of course, by that time, I had lived in Israel for some years, so I knew the correct answer. I said, "Of course, we worship the God of Israel." He said to me, "I just wondered because I hear Christians say they worship God and they sing to God, but there are many gods in this world, and I wondered which one Christians worshipped."

My husband and I traveled all over the world and asked the question above. There was usually dead silence. Then one time in the Far East, a brave voice shyly answered, "The God of Abraham, Isaac, and Jacob?"

For ourselves, we do not cling to any particular denomination but only to the Lord Jesus Himself, with a firm faith in the one true God. We would rather take the end of a sword than deny Jesus (Yeshua), who died for us.

Historical Church

As a child in Sunday school, I was taught to revere and sing "O little town of Bethlehem," to hear about Nazareth where Jesus grew up, and to hear about His walk carrying the cross. These biblical locations have been part of Israel from long ago and remain to this day. Everyone should visit Israel once in their lives.

The church, throughout history, stretched out its hands and asked God to fill them often with material things instead of more of Jesus, who He was, who He is, and who He will forever be. The institutionalized church also used a pious hand against the Jewish people instead of caring for those called the "apple of His eye" (Zechariah 2:8). As the thorny shrub of replacement theology took root and grew quickly in the backyards of Christian churches, hidden as if buried in the ground were treasures found across the landscape.

History and time have uncovered the treasure of blessing. Had Christian history acted upon the Genesis 12:3 covenant that God made regarding the Jewish people "a special treasure above all the peoples who are on the face of the earth" (Deuteronomy 14:2), based upon the collective evidence contained in our history books, the libraries of church history would not be filled with reminders of shameful sins and unspeakable atrocities perpetrated against the sons of Abraham.

Since Bible scholars can easily prove that Christianity is Jewish, a *netzer* ("an offshoot") of the root of David, it behooves us to reconnect to the roots that the church fathers worked diligently to sever. Many church fathers' antisemitic teachings flowed into our churches like a spring filling a dry *wadi* (an old Arabic term for a parched valley), and much of Christendom today is still drinking from that same source.

It has been said that the historical church never totally operated on a genuinely scriptural basis. Therefore, it would seem nearly impossible to reform that which Jesus did not launch. Some branches of Christianity state that what is needed is a restoration to the simplicity of earlier congregations, free from man-made, stately structures controlled by a religious hierarchy. What many do not realize is that the first believers of Yeshua (Jesus) were very Jewish in their form of worship, and many simply met in their homes. The first believers knew nothing of Gothic cathedrals, huge buildings with high steeples, or grandiose sanctuaries.

Typically, anything remotely Jewish is missing from today's Christian worship and study times. Many converts to Christianity married into Greek or Hellenistic households, which eventually led to a clouding of the understanding of His teachings. The Lord's festivals, so beautifully described in the Bible, were replaced by holidays not in the Bible under the guise of warm and fuzzy family times. Some incorporated Santa Claus and the Easter Bunny into our worship services. The feast of the Lord called Passover was viewed by many to be cultish. The observance of Shabbat was changed to "Sun" day, although Jesus had not given instructions for such a practice. The "Edict of Constantine" (AD 321) contradicted to "keep the Sabbath holy" (Exodus 20:8). *Sabbath* means "seventh" and was to be a perpetual observance, including the "stranger who is within your gates" (Exodus 20:10; 31:16).

The Roman Catholic Church still defines itself as infallible and claims to be the only "true" church. In its eyes, if a person desires eternal life, they must become a Catholic believer before death. However, not all Catholic friends believe this, and they realize they are not the only church organization that has donned the acclaim of superiority. History reveals to us that centuries of spiritual darkness regarding the role of the Jewish people in world redemption kept many in the dark in traditional Catholic and Protestant churches.

The Genesis 12:3 principle was lost to church history and buried in the soil of time. The dark historical crevice brought about by the church surely will help us come to grips with our shame once we learn what happened. Our mission must be to welcome *the light that the darkness kept out and let it shine.* Today, we are challenged with the privilege of repairing the damage done through spiritual blindness and ignorance of Scripture.

Someone so brilliantly stated, "We are most blinded, not by things we don't know, but by things we think we know." It simply isn't so that God is finished with the Jewish people or that God has replaced Israel with the church! This statement is heresy in its highest form and must not be continued to be believed in the era we are now entering.

When I was a child, there were very few independent home fellowships or gatherings to attend; however, charismatic meetings began in the 1970s. At that time, the ancient practice of meeting in homes sprang up. We are seeing more of this even in this day and age since the COVID-19 pandemic. Homes were places where we went for Spirit-filled meetings. There was a freedom of worship and joy in the Lord we had never known before. We could raise our hands and even dance in ecstatic joy and concentration on the Lord.

The 1980s brought charismatic teaching centers, campus fellowships, and more home churches. Traditional churches stood stately on corners of streets as a reminder that people had entered "Christian" communities. They remained majestically built and positioned throughout our towns and cities across America. Many Midwestern villages and small towns, such as ours, had a church on nearly every corner.

In the earlier 1900s, my grandmother attended meetings called camp meetings. Sometimes, people labeled those lively assemblies as "holy roller" meetings, but her life totally changed when she met Jesus at one of them. In the late 1990s and following, megachurches arose. I have seen churches in major shopping centers in the Far East with as many as 25,000 in a congregation. Some throughout America had thousands also, all built with congregational finances.

While millions of true believers have been brought out of mostly dead church systems, in the last quarter of the last century, millions of evangelical Christian eyes were opened across the nations as they recognized God's plan for Israel. Books like *The Late Great Planet Earth* by Hal Lindsey guided many of us to realize that as believers in Jesus, we had converted to the God of Israel from paganism and that we were grafted into a Hebrew olive tree.

From Darkness to Light

It was only after May 14, 1948, when the nation of Israel came into being, that the lights in the church began to flicker and then emerge with a steady light. Sometimes cartoons depict when "someone gets it" like a light bulb going on in the brain. Indeed, it was a flash of brilliant light that helped many to see the light.

The church has for centuries proclaimed that Israelites have a veil over their eyes and are blind to Jesus. Conversely, the Jewish people feel the church has a veil over their eyes, not completely seeing who the God of Israel is. Church sanctuary lights had been switched off, and spiritual power had been lost. Then, during the 1970s and 1980s, there was a spiritual awareness of Bible prophecy being fulfilled that focused on the promise and the regathering of the Jews to their homeland. This prophetic fulfillment had been far from the thoughts of the Christian clergy.

From age to age, the Words of a Living God, who is forever unchanging, whose nature is the same yesterday, today, and forever is that solid foundation we need. "But now made manifest, and by the prophetic Scriptures made known to all nations, according to the commandment of the everlasting God, for obedience to the faith" (Romans 16:26).

Yes, thank God, the lights came back on in many places of worship, especially during the last quarter of the last century. When they did, multitudes of Christians became lovers of

Zion, in a great move of the Holy Spirit in America and Europe. The 1970s, 1980s, and 1990s were gloriously revelatory years. As new friends of Israel, with awakened hearts, many of us understood our Hebraic heritage by studying Bible prophecy.

From this modern period of revival came a great spiritual awakening, which changed many lives, and uncountable numbers learned to stand with the nation of Israel. Many Christians who came into the kingdom during those years helped the Jewish nation and its people.

It is meant to be a light in good times and in difficult times. Along with staff and volunteers of Christian Friends of Israel, Ray and I were in Israel during the Gulf War of 1991, when Saddam Hussein's missiles were sent over Israel's borders from Western Iraq. We stood on the frontlines with Israeli soldiers during the Gaza conflict of 2015, right in the dust and dirt of helicopters, along with rockets flying over our heads. The memories are brilliantly clear as we sailed the high seas with the Ebenezer Emergency Fund to bring Jewish people home in the 1990s. Christian Friends of Israel teams flew on Russian Aeroflot aircraft to Belarus and Ukraine to locate some of the Holocaust survivors.

Penetrating the darkness of the former Soviet Union to search for survivors living in prison houses, dodging the KGB, all to uncover the treasures of darkness, was a spiritual battle previously unknown to us. Risking our lives was normal during those years. We never worried about the danger in high-risk places. When the opportunities arose, we seized each assignment as an undertaking God asked us to do for Him and His people. Each mission we undertook was unforgettable and changed our lives forever.

It seems the dark ages are upon us once again. Amid hatred toward the Jews and BDS (Boycott, Divestment and Sanctions, a Palestinian-led movement designed to pressure Israel into making concessions), things have stopped working. It is difficult to get a full grasp of all that is happening so quickly. As in the past, power structures have decayed, as well as societies. Things seem to be on a downward spiral, as once glorious civilizations are being extinguished. Just as the Roman Empire split in two, the dreams of the east and west are quickly separating states, provinces, and people.

Today, unfortunately, antisemitic hatred for the Jewish people is being clocked at a faster rate of thrust than a high-speed train barreling down the railroad tracks. It can be found anywhere you travel in the world today. As a result of this abomination in the eyes of God, we see a downshift in progressive nations. The glory of the nations is disappearing. Unrest, revolutions, and rebellion have stained the topography of nation after nation—all caught in the antisemitic web of deception.

There is an invisible killer among the nations, antisemitism, that just won't die. There seems to be no cure unless one chooses to follow God's Word to bless what He has blessed. The last of

Christian and other nations will retreat into history unless this deadly virus of antisemitism is eliminated. Otherwise, they will become enshrouded in darkness, as in the Middle Ages. Instant Internet, social media, and other forms of modern technology fuel the train of hostility and promote hatred through lies.

God is restoring Israel to her homeland. Gentiles are seeing His light and coming to understand that they are to be a part of His end-time prophecy. The redemption of Israel has been orchestrated by God for His name, which benefits the world. "The Gentiles shall come to your light, And kings to the brightness of your rising" (Isaiah 60:3).

I truly enjoyed my childhood years. Today, when I see so many homes torn apart and the children who do not know which man is their daddy in some homes, I'm so grateful to God that I had a great farming community to grow up in as a child, one that feared God and taught me also to follow Him. The church was the center of our life, much like the synagogue is for a Jewish community. When I was older, I, of course, learned more about Him and came to understand God and what it means to know Him. My desire is for the reader to join us in our pursuit of the God of Abraham, Isaac, and Jacob.

The Pointing of the Finger

> Do not be arrogant toward the branches; but if you are
> arrogant, remember that it is not you who supports the
> root, but the root supports you.
>
> Romans 11:18

If anyone took the angry blows from the dark ages of history, it was the Jewish people. A substantial part of the reason was the shaking of the finger by members of traditional churches with mindsets such as, "You are Christ-killers!" While Christians were not the first antisemites, the early fathers of the church hammered out the "Christ killer" label as in a stone engraving on the Jewish people instead of including all guilty people: "For all have sinned" (Romans 3:23). Why did the church point the finger at the Jewish people as if they alone had crucified Jesus? What about the Romans? What about our sins?

I bring up two thousand years of Christian antisemitic hostility because it took various forms. It was because of those historical blows that the church gave the Jewish people and all the damage done to the Lord's relatives, in His name, that prompted my husband and me to voluntarily uproot from our homeland and put our roots down in Israel. We simply had no idea, until after our arrival, of the extent of the wounds that had been inflicted by our own people over the centuries. It was a rude awakening. Nevertheless, we stayed at our work because we saw that much fallow ground needed to be broken up, obstacles placed on the holy highway to Zion, had to be removed, repair damage done, and the hard ground needed cultivating. We realized that we had to stay among those called to prepare the way to Zion.

We plowed the harsh soil of mistrust, suspicion, and in some cases, actual disgust toward Christians. Upon our arrival, most Israelis didn't want to form friendships. It took years before some of our neighbors spoke to us until...until they were sure that a relationship and genuine friendship could be formed. A nation of people had been deeply wounded. Christians need to know this and adjust their approach to Jewish people accordingly.

Heart-to-heart love and relations.

For over thirty years, the ministry of Christian Friends of Israel has been making a difference in Jewish–Christian relationships, and it has taken unyielding and determined human bonding as well as old-fashioned hard work to repair the damage done in the name of Jesus.

Healing the wounds inflicted on His nation in His name will always be a top priority. It took a lifetime of work before we witnessed trust being re-established. We approached everyone unconditionally, knowing that we were to apply God's healing balm, which was part of the reason God had sent us to the land. It was the medicine we took to everyone to massage broken hearts and heal shattered lives. He was always with us.

Frankly, my life has been enriched by thirty years of living in Israel, among God's people. We must get rid of religious supremacy and approach our Jewish brethren with gracious hearts of mercy and love. Derek Prince always said, "We owe the Jews a great debt." They gave us all that we possess.[13] The Apostle Paul warned us about pride and arrogance in Romans, chapters nine, ten, and eleven. Have we, as a universal body of believers, learned to love anyone unconditionally, wholeheartedly, and without reservation? If so, then why not the Jewish people? This is the only way we are going to be able to sit down and talk with our Jewish brothers and sisters. Otherwise, the breach between us will never be healed.

The earliest members of the followers of Jesus, who were Jewish, met in the Temple to praise God, but gentiles were explicitly excluded from going into the Temple because they came from pagan backgrounds and had worshipped other gods (Acts 2:46). Notice two of Jesus' apostles, Peter and John, are recorded to have gone to the Temple for prayer during the time of the *mincha* (afternoon) prayers: "Now Peter and John were going up to the temple at the hour of prayer, the ninth hour" (Acts 3:1). The ninth hour would have been three o'clock in the afternoon.

Peter's sermon on the Day of Pentecost (*Shavuot*) was entirely Jewish, copiously quoting from the prophets and David. Therefore, it is likely that the 3,000 people who were saved that day would have all been Jewish (Acts 2:1-41).

Some Bible teachers point to Peter as the first accuser of deicide. He pointed right to the religious establishment of Jesus' day.

> Peter, Filled with the Holy Spirit, said to them, "Rulers of the people and elders, if we are being examined today concerning a good deed done to a crippled man [...] let it be known to all of you and to all the people of Israel that by the name of Jesus Christ of Nazareth, whom you crucified [...] by him this man is standing before you well."
>
> Acts 4:8-10

The Catholic Church repented of such accusation in 1964: *The Declaration on the Relation of the Church with Non-*

Christian Religions states that the crucifixion of Jesus "cannot be charged against all Jews, without distinction, then alive, nor against the Jews today."[14] It is a miracle that this statement was made in light of a derogatory statement toward the Torah by the current pope: "It does not offer the fulfillment of the promise because it is not capable of being able to fulfill it."[15]

There were two people groups ready to condemn Christ that day: the Jews and the Romans. While we know that the Sanhedrin decreed His death, only the Roman governor, Pontius Pilate, had the power to execute Jesus to death. Thus, Jesus was scourged, mocked, and crucified as a Jewish religious rebel by the Romans.

Through the centuries, Christianity thought it had a right to tell the Jewish people, "God is finished with you! You are under the law, cursed and going to hell!" If God's mercy saved the gentiles, and Scripture tells us this is true, then we need to realize that it will also be by His mercy that He will save His people.

Caiaphas prophesied that Jesus' death would be for the good of the whole world:

Caiaphas, who was high priest that year said to them, "You know nothing at all, nor do you take into account that it is expedient for you that one man dies for the people and that the whole nation not perish" [...] he did not say this on his own [...] he prophesied that Jesus was going to die for the nation, and that He might gather the children of God from all over the world together as one.

John 11:49-52

Even though the religious of that time rejected Jesus, He, while hanging on the cross, so beautifully said, "Father, forgive them" (Luke 23:34). Oh, the beauty within the Messiah's heart. Let me say right now that if He had not died and become the Lamb of God that took away my sins, I would not be writing this book for you, but I would be lost in my sins, and most likely, pointing my own finger at the very people I am called to love.

The way I look at it, God was pleased that His Son suffered for the redemption of Israel and the world. He sent Him to die for the sins of all. Someone had to offer the spotless Lamb. According to the Torah, Israel's religious authorities were the only ones qualified to do it.

The apostles' ministry continued exclusively among the Jewish people, among whom were thousands who believed and were zealous for the Torah (Acts 21:20). Even after they were imprisoned but miraculously escaped, an angel told them, "Go, stand and speak to the people in the Temple the whole message of this life" (Acts 5:20).

The Gospels are full of examples of rifts between the followers of Jesus and Rabbinic Judaism, which intensified during the Jewish–Roman bloodiest wars, the Bar Kokhba Revolt (AD 132–135). The Jewish sage Rabbi Akiva convinced the Sanhedrin at Yavneh to support the revolt and actually regarded its leader (Simon Bar Kokhba) as the Jewish Messiah. Since the Jewish followers of Jesus could not support such a claim (and therefore could not support the war), the divide between Rabbinical Judaism and the early Jesus Movement, "The Way" (later known as the Christian church), became sealed.

Foundational Scriptures

Most of the early founding fathers of Christianity during the first and second centuries were careful to protect the foundational scriptures entrusted to Israel, beginning with the books of Moses (Torah) through to the major and minor prophets. They possessed the Hebrew scriptures from which the disciples of Jesus taught as they went into other parts of the world with the Gospel after Jesus' resurrection. Not until 382 CE did the universal "church" canonize the "Newer" Testament books containing much of the "Old" Testament scriptures. An article published in the *Jerusalem Post* written by a good friend, Michael Freund, an Orthodox Jew, wrote: "An even deeper problem is the use of the term 'Old Testament,' which suggests that the Hebrew Bible is outdated and archaic like an old shoe or outmoded car that should be discarded."[16] He is precisely correct. The Torah was made for eternity. All of the teachings of Jesus were based upon it. He had not come to abolish it. "Do not even begin to think that I came to destroy the Torah or the Prophets. I did not come with the purpose to cancel them but rather to interpret them properly" (Matthew 5:17, HHB).

The Torah reveals the unconditional covenant that God made with Abraham and his descendants. This truth is missing in the Christian understanding of Israel from an educational perspective of our Hebraic foundations. Many who teach New Testament scriptures have not connected to the proper Hebraic understanding. Misunderstandings have arisen as to the teachings of Rabbi Shaul (the apostle Paul). These misinterpretations often lead to a separation from our Jewish connection.

Gleaning more spiritual meaning behind the history and prophecy of the Hebrew scriptures was practiced by Jewish scholars before Christian scholars emerged. But taken too far, allegorical interpretation of the Hebrew scriptures led to Christians replacing Israel with the church, which is replacement theology. Transferring the blessings of Abraham to the church alone created a path straight to heresy and buried the Jewishness of Jesus. Through the centuries, many church leaders followed the pattern of that type of disconnect, which established enmity between Christians and Jews.

> At the beginning of the third century, Origen of Alexandria introduced to the church an exegetical method that searched for the hidden, spiritual meanings of Old Testament passages, treating the Old Testament as a great allegory of Christ.[17]

He was considered the father of allegory and merged Greek mythology into biblical teaching.[18] The listeners were familiar with Greek mysticism. Therefore, Origen used the familiar to teach the scriptures, a method successfully used today but can be very dangerous if the scriptures are bent to fit our own objective.

> Origen did not invent his interpretive techniques but borrowed them from a complex hermeneutical environment that was already present in his day. These included both Christian and non-Christian elements. Christian influences on his approach to Scripture came from the Bible itself and the precedents set by early Christian interpreters (such as Justin Martyr, Melito and the apostolic fathers, who bequeathed to Origen certain terms and symbols that he adapted and used in his own homilies). On-Christian influences on Origen's exegesis came from Greek, Jewish and heretical sources. Allegorical interpretation was first developed in Hellenism of ancient Greece.[19]

Jesus said that the scriptures testified of Himself (John 5:39). As Christians, we see Christ from the first word to the last. However, care must be given to know when God is speaking specifically to Israel in the context of a sentence. We can, when desired, learn tremendous lessons of faith through their history and share in the blessings of life. However, danger lies in the erasing of the intended application—specifically, to Israel. "Teachers who claim that God has abandoned ethnic Israel are directly impugning the credibility of the Gospel message itself! Yes, it is that serious of an issue."[20]

The Word of God was quite often wrongly handled, and the conscience of the church at one point became seared when it came to protecting, comforting, and taking care of God's chosen people during the Holocaust. It is extremely important that we begin to see the Bible through Jewish eyes and take off our own blinders.

The bottom line for us is that we were birthed from Hebrew stock and must remain attached to our roots as a *netzer*, an offshoot of biblical Judaism, which sprang from the original olive tree (Israel), or we will be cut off. (Romans 11:22). When a congregation begins to be grafted back into its root system, it opens up additional spiritual blessings to be poured out. Christians do not need to become Jewish to love Israel. We just need to be in the right relationship with her and be a blessing as commanded by God.

Stop Being Jewish

One of the greatest errors of the church, and which makes me very contemplative about the seriousness of this matter, was when the church misled the Jewish people by trying to take them away from what God commanded them as a chosen people and a Jewish nation, in forcing them to renounce the commandments of God for them as prescribed in the Torah as was done during the Holocaust.

The historical church took most rights away from Jews. They told them that they could not worship on Shabbat, must eat nonkosher foods, forsake God's festivals, nor could they participate in most normalcies of life without conversion.[21]

This is a grave sin in the eyes of God, who commanded Jews to follow His commands and rules. "So the sons of Israel shall observe the sabbath, to celebrate the sabbath throughout their generations as a perpetual covenant" (Exodus 31:16). One of the meanings of "perpetual" is "forever." There is also a blessing upon gentiles who observe the Sabbath:

Also the foreigners who join themselves to the LORD, To minister to Him, and to love the name of the LORD, To be His servants, everyone who keeps from profaning the Sabbath And holds fast My covenant; Even those I will bring to My holy mountain And make them joyful in My house of prayer. Their burnt offerings and their sacrifices will be acceptable on My altar; For My house will be called a house of prayer for all the peoples.

Isaiah 56:6-7

In all my years of studies and teaching about Israel and the church, I rarely encountered a Christian who was ashamed of how the historical church morally wronged the Jewish people in their most significant time of need; only a few showed remorse.

I've seen no one shaking their heads in shame and disgust. Along with a remnant who feared God, and acted nobly, lay those who could not find their conscience in a time of great danger and human depravity for the Jews.

Parts of this spiritual puzzle, in my own mind, still need to be put into place to form a better picture of how anyone, who made the sign of the cross, or was a "man of the collar," those who wore ecclesiastical robes and those who confessed a traditional Christian creed, could be so hard-hearted as to assist the Nazis as accomplices and still call themselves "disciples of Christ."

It was totally against everything the Messiah stood for. It is our natural inclination to go easy on church history toward the Jewish people. While I do not wish to judge nor slander anyone's character during the centuries or presently, the church's shortcomings make clear the damage done. The hiding of any wrongdoing and pretending that there is nothing to talk about here furthers the damage in the hearts of many of my Jewish friends about how the church acted during various periods of history toward them. The desire to look impressive while inside the palms of the hands are stained with blood could only allow history to be repeated. We all want to be clean before the Lord.

When we first moved to Israel, I decided to crack the history books as much as possible to understand the negative responses I received from some of the Jewish people who questioned our presence in the land. Once I realized what had been done, I was able to see more clearly what Christians needed to do to correct the errors of the centuries and be able to tear down walls and repair damage done in order to be a genuine witness of Jesus. It's His name I wish to represent, not that of religion. I love my Christian brethren too much to remain silent. I so desire to be sensitive when bringing to the surface what the historical church did to Israel that, sometimes, it is difficult to write about.

The complete bloodstained history of the Russian pogroms under the czars, Christendom's Crusaders, who were against everyone who did not follow their religion or did not look like them, used their swords and shields with huge crosses as weapons against the Jewish people. The directives that were given to harm the Jewish people still echo down the corridors of time. If ever I meet one Christian antisemite, I will ask, "Why did you do it?"

History recorded the Christian Nazi sympathizers wore the symbol of the cross around their necks. They also went to church on Christmas Eve and sang of baby Jesus. Often singing the hymns of the church, they donned their coats and went to the nearest concentration camp to aid in the killing of Jews.[22] In time, I also learned that many Nazis wore belt buckles monogrammed with "God with Us," stating that they were following the true God and that He had ordered them to kill all the Jews. It genuinely causes me much consternation at those "unthinkable" actions.

Did they not know that they were defying Jesus? Most likely, because the nationality of Christ was never taught, they never thought about Jesus being a Jew in the flesh; otherwise, why would they do the exact opposite of what He taught? Jesus' words "love thy neighbor as yourself" (Matthew 22:39) expressed His will. He never said, "Love thy neighbor as thyself unless they are Jewish."

What happened to the reasoning and thought processes of those "Sunday-go-to-meeting" people who committed unthinkable crimes of apathy and indifference toward the Jews? And now, Christianity wants to know why the Jewish people reject its gospel of "love" that displayed an unrelenting gospel of hate to them?

The proof of the guilty-as-charged judgment came home personally to me. Upon our arrival in Israel in 1985, while visiting the home of a Holocaust survivor from a European death camp, she looked at me in amazement. She said, "Why would you want to help me?" In other words, "Christians don't help Jews!"

I was taken aback but did not yet realize the full extent of the reason behind her question. I had to learn why she felt so resentful and indignant toward me. It had only been forty years (1985) since she had been liberated from the perpetual suffering and evil of Hitler's Nazi Germany. The wounds were not yet closed but still felt recent within her mind of how Christian "neighbors" looked the other way.

The years of the Holocaust (1933–1945) were when the faithful disappeared from the sons of men, and few responded to godliness. They slept the sleep of death as their eyes were not enlightened (Psalm 12:1; 13:3). The saddest thing about it all, Christianity carried His name! "Bear My Name before the Gentiles, and kings, and the children of Israel" (Acts 9:15).

That era seems to be one of the most difficult times to understand how an apostate church, who acted parallel to Orpah, the sister-in-law of Ruth, turned its head and walked away from Naomi. If Jesus were on earth today, judging the sheep and goat nations (Matthew 24:32), I could envision Him saying to those who betrayed the Jews, "depart from me, I never knew you" (Matthew 7:23).

I want to make clear that some of these people who committed horrendous sins toward the Jewish people were very educated, highly professional scholars, and I'm sure highly creative and likable people when meeting them. So what went wrong? I truly believe it was the teachings they had been sitting under which had its feet solidly on the ground of replacement theology, which goes directly against what the Bible teaches.

The damage done to separate our faiths can begin to mend just by accepting all that God says about Israel, her past, and future. I am most hopeful for my people in the worldwide movement of true followers of Jesus. God forbid we ever let the Jewish people down again!

The Power to Choose

> I call heaven and earth as witnesses today against you, that I have set before your life and death, blessing and cursing; therefore choose life, that both you and your descendants may live.
>
> Deuteronomy 30:19

Derek Prince was a pioneer teacher on the subject of blessings and curses, which had a tremendous, lasting impact. My husband, Ray, and I were, personally, richly blessed to have known the late, well-known international Bible scholar, teacher, and author. He was one of the most outstanding teachers we have ever known and instrumental in Christian Friends of Israel (CFI's) foundations. His counsel, along with Reverend Lance Lambert's, an international author and teacher, and Freda Lindsay's of Christ for the Nations Bible College, was invaluable.

I will always cherish having been asked by Derek to drive him to the hospital when his wife, Ruth, was so ill. I sat with each of them to hold their hand before they were taken to glory. However, Hannah Ben Haim is the real heroine, as she cared for Derek in her own home. I'm just glad to have had a small part in providing for their welfare. Derek taught that the two opposing powers of blessings and curses influence one's life either to yield fruit for God's kingdom or to fail to receive blessings that could have been.[23]

Ray and I, while traveling in European countries, would, on certain occasions, take time out from ministry to locate Jewish cemeteries wherever we could find them. Once pinpointed, we found them mostly in neglected and poor condition and buried in the abandoned soil of puzzling events that had surrounded the Jewish people. Every gravestone would give some aspect of information about the life buried there. Likewise, the graveyards of church cemeteries around the world are filled with stone monuments, which represent individuals who perhaps had to make a choice one way or another with Jewish people.

The Lord places choices before us to test our mettle. Most of us go through life totally ignorant of the two forces: blessings and curses. As Derek suggested, we need to understand there are consequences for the choices we make. With each, it can mean life or destruction. While concentrating intensively on Bible studies over the years, I began to notice similarities in passages, a uniformity of end results that positively affected non-Jewish lives when presented with an opportunity to bless a Jewish person.

Throughout Scripture, we have examples of gentiles, including their names and circumstances, who blessed the chosen people. The preceding accounts were sufficiently noteworthy for God to memorialize them in His everlasting Word. The narrative helped open my eyes. It is a standard for those who wish to obey God.

To be blessed with the wisdom to make the right choices should be the aspiration of every individual's journey upon the earth, but sometimes making the right choice can be difficult. Asking God for His help to live righteously and have his promises operating in our life will bring real joy and peace. Conversely, choosing to ignore God's promises has consequences that can be costly.

> Behold, I set before you today a blessing and a curse: the
> blessing, if you obey the commandments of the LORD
> your God which I command you today; and the curse,
> if you do not obey the commandments of the LORD
> your God.
>
> Deuteronomy 11:26-28

The story of Balaam, a soothsayer from the land of Mesopotamia, provides a biblical example of one who ultimately caused Israel to stumble through his wicked counsel. Balaam was hired by Balak, a Moabite king, to curse his enemy, Israel. Balak knew the forty-year history of God's people and was terrified of what they could do to him. "Now this company will lick up everything around us, as an ox licks up the grass of the field" (Numbers 22:4). Balak could be considered a model of arrogance, which, unfortunately, depicts the historical church, which for 2,000 years has exhibited spiritual pride regarding the Jewish people.

Persuaded by wealth, Balaam tried to please Balak but was not allowed by God to curse Israel for any price: "And God came to Balaam at night and said to him, 'If the men come to call you, rise and go with them; but only the word which I speak to you—that you shall do'" (Numbers 22:20).

"How shall I curse whom God has not cursed? And how shall I denounce whom the LORD has not denounced?" (Numbers 23:8). Therefore, Balaam blessed Israel four times with words similar to those God spoke to Abraham.

Balaam's Blessings

For from the top of the rocks I see him, and from the hills I behold him; There! A people dwelling alone, Not reckoning itself among the nations. "Who can count the dust of Jacob, Or number one-fourth of Israel? Let me die the death of the righteous, and let my end be like his."

Numbers 23:9-10

He has not observed iniquity in Jacob, nor has He seen wickedness in Israel. The LORD his God is with him, And the shout of a King is among them [...] For there is no sorcery against Jacob, nor any divination against Israel [...] It shall not lie down until it devours the prey, And drinks the blood of the slain.

Numbers 23:21-24

How lovely are your tents, O Jacob! Your dwellings, O
Israel! Like valleys that stretch out [...] He shall pour
water from his buckets, and his seed shall be in many
waters [...] And his kingdom shall be exalted.

Numbers 24:5-7

I see Him, but not now; I behold Him, but not near;
A Star shall come out of Jacob; A Scepter shall rise out
of Israel, and batter the brow of Moab, and destroy all
the sons of tumult. Edom shall be a possession; Seir
also, his enemies, shall be a possession, While Israel does
valiantly. Out of Jacob One shall have dominion, and
destroy the remains of the city.

Numbers 24:17-19

Balaam spoke the words the Lord gave him, but his heart was
full of malice and greed. He intended to curse Israel and tried
his best to do so. Some scholars believe the blessings Balaam
spoke over Israel were inadvertent—an example of a man who
misused religious authority for his own profit. Jude, author of
the Epistle by his name, says, "Woe to them! For they have gone
in the way of Cain, have run greedily in the error of Balaam for
profit" (Jude 1:11). The "error of Balaam" was that he pursued
profit rather than obeying the Lord.

Balaam, the man who "sees the vision of the Almighty
[...] with eyes wide open," did not see as clearly as his donkey
(Numbers 24:4). May the Lord open our eyes, and may we

avoid the error of Balaam: greed and spiritual pride.

The wicked Balaam knew that Israel was invincible as long as the Israelites preserved the holiness of God. So, instead, "through the counsel of Balaam," the Moabite women enticed the Israelite men into idolatry and sexual perversion (Numbers 31:16). As a result, God sent a plague among the congregation of the Lord, and 24,000 Jews died.

It makes me cringe when I think of how the historical church, like Balaam, wanted Israel to turn from God's laws and stop being Jewish. In Revelation 2:14, the church at Pergamos was rebuked because they held to the doctrine of Balaam, which caused the Jewish people to stumble, leading them astray.

A strict warning in Scripture advises us against trying to change what God has commanded His Jewish people to follow:

> But I have a few things against you because you have there those who hold the doctrine of Balaam, who taught Balak to put a stumbling block before the children of Israel, to eat things sacrificed to idols, and to commit sexual immorality.
>
> Revelation 2:14

Ultimately, Balaam's poor judgment resulted in his death because he chose to bring harm instead of blessings to the Israelites (Joshua 13:22).

> Therefore prophesy concerning the land of Israel [...]
> Thus says the Lord GOD: "Behold, I have spoken in my

jealousy and My fury, because you have borne the shame of the nations" [...] Therefore thus says the Lord GOD: "I have raised My hand in an oath that surely the nations that are around you shall bear their own shame."

Ezekiel 36:6-7

In the world to come (*Olam Haba* in Hebrew), Jewish sages declare that each person will be asked to review how he or she lived their time on earth. God's Book of Life and every recorded deed will become either our treasure or cobs and coal.

How many great men of God have given themselves to teach the scriptures but did not really understand them? The book of James, chapter three, offers a sobering explanation:

With it [*the tongue*] we bless our God and Father, and with it we curse men, who have been made in the similitude of God. Out of the same mouth proceed blessing and cursing. My brethren, these things ought not to be so.

James 3:9-10 (hereinafter, brackets added)

The reformer, Martin Luther, is an example of how people of God can do great good and then make a terrible choice and get off the righteous path. Everyone is capable of being deceived if we do not rightly divide the whole Word of God. In his later life, Luther wrote *On the Jews and Their Lies*, a thesis based on his hatred for the people God created to

75

establish His name and bring forth His salvation to the world, the Jews[24].

It is clear that a great man who forged the Protestant Church became arrogant against the Jewish people—the very thing the apostle Paul warned against in Romans 11:18. How can one bless God and hate His people? It was a subtle deception that misguided men have been caught in throughout history. This fuel has kept the fires of antisemitism in the church burning in an ongoing blazing battle for centuries.

The choice to bless requires mercy. The mercy we receive depends upon the mercy given, especially to the people of Israel. Do we believe that because some Jews have rejected Jesus, they are permanently cut off? Dr. Eli Lizorkin-Eyzenberg explains the Hebrew words for "cut off" are actually mistranslated and should be read as "But if some of the branches were bent (or partially broken)," the new branches are grafted in among the branches that are wounded and need special care.[25]

The apostle Paul clearly explained that Israel's inclusion into God's plan of mercy is life from the dead "that through the mercy shown you they also may obtain mercy. For God has committed them all to disobedience, that He might have mercy on all" (Romans 11:15, 31-32).

Unfortunately, much of the church world has wrongly chosen to believe they are Israel's replacement. Many curses have been spoken over the Jewish people because of the unbiblical teaching that God cut them off. It is, in fact, the gentiles who are "cut off" if they do not treat the Jewish people with God's mercy as He has treated non-Jews with mercy, according to Romans 11:22. We must rethink what has been handed down through the channels of time as the Gospel. We must speak what God decreed regarding Israel's rebuilding and return of His people to be blessed.

Valley of Decision

Our mindset toward Israel will shape our actions. My hope is that those reading this book will choose not to remain in theological error. Those who do choose error will be judged accordingly. God will bring Israel's opposers to the Valley of Decision (also called the Valley of Jehoshaphat) for their actions that caused harm to the Jewish people and divided their land (Joel 3:2). Would we dare want to be in that category?

The church should have learned from Matthew, chapter twenty-five, that humanity cannot be blessed and cursed simultaneously. One simply cannot love Jesus and not love the Jewish people. It would be a spiritual dichotomy.

The parable of Jesus in Matthew, chapter twenty-five, clearly states that those who feed and clothe "my brethren" will enter into eternal life. In contrast, those who do not show kindness actually reject Christ and enter into everlasting punishment as it would be "as if it were done unto Him" (Matthew 25:40-46).

However, there is one point important to understand what Jesus meant by "my brethren." A Greek translation states it as "brothers," while the New Revised Standard Version translates it as "members of my family." In the Complete Jewish Bible, it is translated as "these brothers of mine." Another version renders "brothers from the womb." A brother can mean having the same natural ancestor, belonging to the same people, countrymen, or fellow believers.

According to my friend, Claire Pfann, the term "brethren" was not used in Jesus' time by gentiles.[26] It was only used among the Jewish community between one another. Also, the term "brethren" in ancient Israel could not have meant those who were members of the "church" because, at that period of time, there was no "church." To reemphasize, Jesus was specifically referring to His brethren (literally, the Jewish people), who would be facing terrible persecution at the hands of the nations (including harassment by Christian communities).

The Jewish people were told how to receive blessings: to obey God's voice. They have been a people that understand blessings. Blessing the family is part of the Shabbat meal every Friday night in Judaism. The Jewish people bless newborns, young people, soldiers, feast days, etc. They practice "the blessing" and have been a blessing to the world as a result in all fields of academia, finance, agriculture...the list goes on. They also forfeited the blessing through disobedience and idolatry. Circumspectly, the blessing returns after repentance. It was prophesied through Moses that Israel would sin and be sent into the nations and be punished but would return.[27]

If any of you are driven out to the farthest parts under heaven, from there the LORD your God will gather you, and from there He will bring you. Then the LORD your God will bring you to the land which your fathers possessed, and you shall possess it. He will prosper you and multiply you more than your fathers. [...] The LORD your God will make you abound in all the work of your hand, in the fruit of your body, in the increase of your livestock, and in the produce of your land for good. For the LORD will again rejoice over you for good as He rejoiced over your fathers, if you obey the voice of the LORD your God, to keep His commandments and His statutes which are written in this Book of the Law, and if you turn to the LORD your God with all your heart and with all your soul.

Deuteronomy 30:4-5, 9-10

Perhaps, it will help to understand, maybe for the first time, that Christianity forfeited countless spiritual blessings throughout the ages because it rejected God's Torah and Jewish Scriptures taught by Jesus and His disciples. For some, these treasures are being brought back to life for the church. Let's exchange an egocentric gospel for a gospel according to the real teachings of Jesus.

In the Book of Exodus, we learn that after 400 years of Egyptian bondage, the children of Israel were led by Moses out of Egypt to the promised land (Canaan). Joshua (*Yehoshua* in Hebrew or *Yahweh* means "salvation") was his constant companion. He became the leader of the Israelite tribes after Moses died. Joshua had a righteous love for God and His people, and under his leadership, the Israelites conquered most of Canaan.

> Now Joshua built an altar to the LORD God of Israel in Mount Ebal [...] And there, in the presence of the children of Israel, he wrote on the stones a copy of the law of Moses, which he had written. [...] And afterward he read all the words of the law, the blessings and the curses, according to all that is written in the Book of the Law.
>
> Joshua 8:30, 32, 34

Joshua did his best to help Israel become an obedient nation. Israel always had the choice to obey or disobey. The consequence of their disobedience was harsh. Even though God punished His children severely for the sake of His name, He still showed them mercy (Isaiah 40:2, 48:9).

The Israelites were entrusted with much, but they were exiled not once but twice because of sin. They were exiled to Babylon in 587 BC. Then, after the AD 70 Roman destruction, they were scattered among the nations. Eighteen hundred years passed before God began the restoration of returning the Jews back to their homeland, Israel.

The Bible foretold that the gentiles would be part of Israel's restoration.

> The sons of foreigners shall build up your walls, and their kings shall minister to you; for in My wrath I struck you, But in My favor I have had mercy on you. Therefore your gates shall be open continually; They shall not be shut day or night, that men may bring to you the wealth of the Gentiles, and their kings in procession. For the nation and kingdom which will not serve you shall perish, and those nations shall be utterly ruined.
>
> Isaiah 60:10-12

Accepting this scriptural truth immediately directs the church or individual to the pathway of blessing. Contrarily, God might certainly have a serious problem with any nation that curses Israel or His people "For it is the day of the LORD's vengeance, the year of recompense for the cause of Zion" (Isaiah 34:8).

Some may argue that God is unjust; however, God is incapable of injustice. He adamantly states that we will be blessed as we bless Israel. Yeshua clearly spoke to the Samaritan woman at the well an absolute truth. He wanted her to know, "Salvation is of the Jews" (John 4:22). How much clearer could He have made it?

It has been said that reciprocity is God's blessings being given in return to anyone who blesses what He has blessed, in this case, Israel. It is not the old proverbial expression of "one hand washes the other," or backscratching, or any other catchy phrase. Instead, it is purely God's desire to bless not only Israel but also bless anyone else who touches Israel with a godly action or response.

The truth remains firm, but many lack spiritual discernment. If a man can have scales fall from his eyes, like the apostle Paul, or blind people made to see, then a right understanding is possible. One has to be willing to step "out of the box" and visit new lands of biblical understanding just beyond the borders of embedded traditions. The Master will eventually require it for acceptance into the eternal kingdom, as each of the twelve gates has over its entrance the names of the twelve tribes. Take a moment to think about this, please: "Also she had a great and high wall with twelve gates, and twelve angels at the gates, and names written on them, which are [the names] of the twelve tribes of the children of Israel" (Revelation 21:12).

It is said that a dichotomy exists between nations that have blessed Israel and those that have cursed her. For those who have blessed Israel, we see prosperity and a future. Those who have cursed or harmed Israel see her as a problem for the whole world. "In Israeli parlance, this is called 'mowing the grass,' an apt metaphor, as their problems always grow back."[28]

Ahuva Balofsky, a writer for an Israeli news service, recently asked the question, "Are anti-Israel churches cursed?" She then quoted the Genesis 12:3 principle. Ahuva stated that church denominations had put Him (God) to the test by supporting modern Israel's enemies and denouncing the Jewish state. It does seem that there is indeed a price to pay, as numerous churches and denominations are reporting declining numbers.

The Boycott, Divestment, and Sanctions (BDS) movement is quite strong in the American United Church of Christ (UCC) and the United Methodist Church (UMC), to name two of the ten in the *Washington Report on Middle East Affairs*.[29] Support for Israel is considered stronger among evangelicals than traditional denominations. The countries where there are few Jews and those who consider themselves "enlightened" among the educated lean toward BDS as well[30] (Joffe, 2019). These few examples are of those who have chosen poorly in light of God's voice to the world.

Therefore all those who devour you shall be devoured; and all your adversaries, every one of them, shall go into captivity; those who plunder you shall become plunder, And all who prey upon you I will make a prey.

Jeremiah 30:16

O seed of Abraham His servant, you children of Jacob, His chosen ones! [...] He permitted no one to do them wrong; yes, He rebuked kings for their sakes, Saying, "Do not touch My anointed ones, And do My prophets no harm."

Psalm 105:6, 14-15

The dangerous and malignant disease of antisemitism can be cured by knowing that God's blessing rested upon Shem, Noah's son, and his descendants. According to Genesis 9:9, 26, all who would touch Shem's descendants, the children of Israel, would be blessed in a righteous way.

It is time to put our homes in order. The Christian Church can experience a new spiritual reformation and begin to align worldwide with Israel and the Jewish people, according to God's will. God's Word will certainly come to pass regarding those who choose to bless His chosen people. It is true that many nations despise the Jewish people and hate Israel. I yearn to see the day when all the earth will become a blessing to Israel rather than a curse and true peace—a reality.

Legacies of Kindness to the Jew

Do not lay up for yourselves treasures on earth, where
moth and rust destroy and where thieves break in and
steal; but lay up for yourselves treasures in heaven, where
neither moth nor rust destroys and where thieves do not
break in and steal. For where your treasure is, there your
heart will be also.

Matthew 6:19-21

In tracing the route to the path leading to blessing, which
includes the principle and the promise of Genesis 12:3, we need
to ask ourselves if we are meditating carefully about following
scriptural examples of gentiles who responded to Jewish people
with acts of kindness and compassion. We will examine the
results of moral and righteous decisions to determine the end
result which followed each decision.

In some cases from ancient times, gentiles who chose to
be a blessing may have known about the command to bless
God's people from the scrolls of the Torah. Perhaps, they
comprehended how God acted favorably, often miraculously,
toward the chosen people and unfavorably toward those who
caused them harm.

Each Bible story took place during different periods, in
various locations, and with people from different backgrounds
and cultures. The accounts are not out-of-date stories from
the past but living proof that the principle was in operation in

yesterday's ancient biblical world and is still in effect today. In the land of Israel, the soil continually reveals buried treasures, and they testify to Israel's rich history of influence in the centuries before us.

The land owned by churches in many nations also reveals, hypothetically speaking, hidden treasures sometimes buried in the archives or hidden away for centuries. There is a treasure trove of spiritual identification with the Jewish people, which also gives evidence to Christianity's missing link, Israel. The problem is these spiritual riches have been hidden for an incredibly long period of time. Now seems to be the right time to unearth that which has been neglected and forgotten, perhaps, because of spiritual pride and arrogance over the centuries in relation to personal knowledge of Israel, God's "special treasure" (Deuteronomy 7:6, NLT).

As Christians, our Rabbi and Lord, Yeshua, taught us to lay up treasures in heaven. The Jewish sages tell us that a good deed is like giving charity to the needy. That good deed is called a *mitzvah* and literally means "commandment."

Every time we act on a commandment, it is a "good deed." The word *mitzvah* came to be closely associated with acts of goodness. We all have a relatively short lifetime on earth. Our opportunities to bless are limited. The world outside our doors may say, "You can't take it with you"; however, the Bible says that we can. By blessing others, particularly the Jewish people, we invest our resources, our time, and kindness into heavenly things that are on God's heart. We store up either good deeds or evil deeds. Of course, this pertains to any human being; however, we are focusing in this book on seeking the welfare of the Jewish people according to God's Word.

God knows each intent of the deeds and will reward accordingly. When we do not bless the Jewish people and humble ourselves, our heart's pride is lifted up against God's will. The result is a curse. Since God has commanded His blessing upon the nation of Israel, and we owe a tremendous spiritual debt to them, it should be easy for us to say "thank you."

The early gentile church in Macedonia and Achaia understood this principle: "It pleased them indeed, and they are their debtors. If the Gentiles have been partakers of their spiritual things, their duty is also to minister to them in material things" (Romans 15:27).

I hope you will notice in your Bible as you study the model these people chose, who, out of compassion, kindness, and fear of God, blessed the Jewish people and the blessing they received in return. Enjoy the tour around the hall of fame as you pause at different intervals to think about how you would have responded if you had been in their situation. From the rubble of time, these chapters unearth narratives of individual heroic actions. Whether they knew it or not, they were putting into effect the principle and the promise of Genesis 12:3.

Abimelech

> And it came to pass at that time that Abimelech and Phichol, the commander of his army, spoke to Abraham, saying, "God is with you in all that you do. Now therefore, swear to me by God that you will not deal falsely with me, with my offspring, or with my posterity; but that according to the kindness that I have done to you, you will do to me and to the land in which you have dwelt."
>
> Genesis 21:22-23

Abraham was from the great and populous city of Ur, and therefore, a gentile who became the first Hebrew. He was a rough, simple, and venerable Bedouin-like sheep master. Yet, in the long list of Bible saints, he alone is spoken of as "the father of the faithful" and as "the friend of God" (Isaiah 41:8).

During his sojourning at Gerar, a chief city of the Philistines, Abraham pretended that his wife, Sarah, was his sister (Genesis 20:2). A heathen king of the Philistine country, Abimelech, took Sarah with intent to make her one of his wives. But God rebuked Abimelech in a dream (Genesis 20:3, 17). After the king subsequently learned Sarah was not Abraham's sister but his wife, he reproved Abraham for intending to deceive him. What a humiliation it must have been for Abraham to be reprimanded by a pagan ruler. And yet, Abimelech still blessed him and dealt generously with him, loading him down with presents as well as granting him liberty in the land (Genesis 20:14-15).

The blessing, which Abimelech bestowed upon Abraham secured his goodwill. The king and his servants realized that God was with Abraham in all he was doing (Genesis 20:14; 21:22; 26:28; Isaiah 8:3).

When contention arose between the servants of the two men over wells of water, Abimelech and Abraham made a covenant with each other at the well, which was named Beersheva. Before the covenant was sealed between the men, Abimelech expressed concern in his heart for himself and his family's safety and security. He needed reassuring Abraham would return the same kindness to him that he had given to Abraham: "According to the kindness that I have done to you" (Genesis 21: 23).

Abimelech's kindness to Abraham came back to him in the form of abundant blessings through Abraham's prayer to God for the king. God healed Abimelech, his wife, his maidservants—the blessing of having children was granted to him and his household. Favor will return to the one who has given kindness to Abraham's descendants. The promise was, "Abraham shall surely become a great and mighty nation, and all the nations of the earth shall be blessed in him" (Genesis 18:18).

Joseph and Potiphar

Now Joseph had been taken down to Egypt. And Potiphar, an officer of Pharaoh, captain of the guard, an Egyptian, bought him from the Ishmaelites who had taken him down there. The LORD was with Joseph, and he was a successful man; and he was in the house of his master the Egyptian. And his master saw that the LORD was with him and that the LORD made all he did to prosper in his hand. So Joseph found favor in his sight, and served him. Then he made him overseer of his house, and all that he had he put under his authority. So it was, from the time that he had made him overseer of his house and all that he had, that the LORD blessed the Egyptian's house for Joseph's sake; and the blessing of the LORD was on all that he had in the house and in the field.

Genesis 39:1-5

Joseph was a favored son by his father, Jacob, and by God, which incited his brothers to jealousy. To rid themselves of "the dreamer," his brothers sold Joseph to Ishmaelites, who took him to Egypt. Potiphar, captain of the pharaoh's army, bought Joseph from them (Genesis 39:1). Despite his brothers' betrayal and subsequent slavery, Joseph prospered in all he did, which did not go unnoticed.

We learn that the Lord was with Joseph. It was perhaps an invisible hand of God that guided Potiphar, the high Egyptian officer, to bring him into his private dwelling. He quickly approved, trusted, and promoted Joseph. It was then that the Lord blessed Potiphar in return. In determining that God was with Joseph (a son of the Hebrew nation), Potiphar's favorable actions toward him prompted the blessings to flow in his own life and household.

Falsely accused by Potiphar's wife, Joseph finds himself in a prison cell. Still, he prospered. God's blessings promoted Joseph to second in command to the prison guard. He continued to use his gifts and managed things well, knowing that God had a plan for his life.

Joseph interpreted dreams, one of which was the pharaoh's (Genesis 41:26), which told of Egypt's future as provider during a far-reaching, seven-year famine. In turn, Joseph's dreams, given to him by God during his youth, came to pass. His brothers and father indeed bowed down to him (Genesis 37:7). God used Joseph to provide for Israel in the land of Egypt. The promise was, "They are beloved for the sake of the fathers. For the gifts and the calling of God are irrevocable" (Romans 11:28-29).

Jethro

"Then Jethro rejoiced for all the good which the LORD had done for Israel, whom He had delivered out of the hand of the Egyptians" (Exodus 18:9).

Jethro, Moses's father-in-law, was a righteous gentile who merited recognition for his contribution to the Israelites during their Exodus journey. He openly recognized God's deliverance and miracles for the Hebrew people.

To avoid confusion as much as possible, consider that the Torah used several names for Jethro. Each of the names found in *Strong's Concordance* speaks of Jethro's good character:

> Reul (Exodus 2:18): a friend of God;
> Jethro (Exodus 3:1): His abundance;
> Jether (Exodus 4:18): abundant;
> Putiel (Exodus 6:25): afflicted by God;
> Hobab (Numbers 10:29): cherished.

Jethro, a member of the Kenite tribe (Exodus 3:1; Judges 1:16) and priest of Midian, expressed reverence and worship for the one true God.[31] Jethro and Moses had a special bond and trusted each other. Jethro is an important person we read about in the Torah. Not just the father of Moses's wife, but also one used by God to help Moses and the children of Israel along the way.

Moses asked his father-in-law's permission to depart from his responsibilities with him in order to lead the children of Israel out of Egypt. Jethro said to Moses, "Go in peace" (Exodus 4:18). Jethro recognized a higher calling for his son-in-law and did not prevent him from doing God's will.

Sometimes later, Jethro brought Zipporah, Moses's wife, and her two sons to the Israelite camp at the Mount of God. After a warm greeting, Moses told him of all the mighty works of the Lord, which delighted Jethro.

> Now I know that the LORD is greater than all gods: for in the thing wherein they dealt proudly he was above them. And Jethro, Moses' father in law, took a burnt

offering and sacrifices for God: and Aaron came, and all
the elders of Israel, to eat bread with Moses' father in law
before God.

Exodus 18:11-12

Jethro taught Moses an effective judicial system that helped
meet the people's demands for justice when they quarreled with
each other that consequently contributed to the well-being of
Moses (Exodus 18:17-24). The wisdom he gave helped relieve
Moses from being overburdened by the people's conflicts.

While there can appear to be an identity confusion between
Numbers 10:29, Judges 1:16 and 4:11, many understand that
Jethro became a guide to help Israel across the wilderness and that
"He and his family converted and joined the Jewish people."[32]

"Now the children of the Kenite, Moses' father-in-law,
went up from the City of Palms with the children of Judah into
the Wilderness of Judah [...] and they went and dwelt among
the people" (Judges 1:16). Jethro was a valuable support and
comfort to Moses. His kindness shown to the Israelites has
special merit yet to be fully appreciated.

Rahab the Harlot

"Now therefore, I pray you, swear unto me by the LORD,
since I have shewed you kindness, that you will also show
kindness unto my father's house, and give me a true token"
(Joshua 2:12, KJV). "Only Rahab the harlot shall live, she and
all who are with her in the house, because she hid the messengers

that we sent" (Joshua 6:17). "By faith the harlot Rahab did not perish with those who did not believe, when she had received the spies with peace" (Hebrews 11:31).

Israel arrived at the gateway of their promised land, Jericho. The first encounter with one of this fortified city's inhabitants was Rahab. Of questionable reputation, she favorably greeted the Hebrew spies and played an important role in Israel's triumph.

"It has been suggested that the word 'harlot' can be translated as 'Innkeeper,' thus making Rahab the landlady of a wayside tavern," meaning she may not have been a harlot as supposed.[33] The meaning of the name *Rahab* is commonly known in Hebrew as "quarrelsome or proud." Perhaps, this gave her the courage and strength she needed for the moment.

Obviously, Rahab, to some degree, believed in the God of Israel. She feared Him enough to help the Hebrew spies by hiding them in her dwelling at the risk of her life during a very uncertain time.

Upon entering Jericho to sack and destroy it, the Hebrew warriors identified Rahab's living quarters by the scarlet cord, which hung from her window (Joshua 2:18).

And the young men who had been spies went in and brought out Rahab, her father, her mother, her brothers, and all that she had. So they brought out all her relatives and left them outside the camp of Israel.

Joshua 6:23

Rahab and her family were taken to safety so that the city could be burned to complete destruction (6:24). Bravely contributing to the well-being of the Jewish people is recognized and rewarded by God.

Rahab lived among the Hebrews from that time on and was probably the one named in the linage of Jesus. Her placement in the hall of fame recorded in the book of Hebrews was because of her faith in the God of Israel. The promise was given "In the same way, Rachab the prostitute was justified by works... just as the body without the spirit is dead, so also faith without corresponding actions is dead" (James 2:25-26, HHB).

Caleb

Now therefore, give me this mountain of which the LORD spoke in that day; for you heard in that day how the Anakim were there, and that the cities were great and fortified. It may be that the LORD will be with me, and I shall be able to drive them out as the LORD said.

Joshua 14:12

Caleb, of the tribe of Judah, was one of the two spies who gave a positive testimony about the promised land. "We are well able to take the land," was his report, while the ten negative spies saw themselves as small and unable to come against the inhabitants of the land that God had promised. The doubting people listened to the ten spies and became afraid, which greatly displeased the

Lord. Therefore, only Caleb and Joshua were allowed to receive the promise to the first generation. "But My servant Caleb, because he has had a different spirit and has followed Me fully, I will bring into the land which he entered, and his descendants shall take possession of it" (Numbers 14:24).

Moses had promised Caleb the portion of land known as Hebron (Joshua 14:10-15); significant to the Israelites because it was where Abraham had lived and was buried. This burial site, the Cave of Machpelah, was the first parcel of land owned by the Hebrew people purchased by Abraham as a burial place for Sarah (Genesis 23:19).

In ancient times, Hebron was known as Kiriath Arba, after Arba (progenitor of the giants of Canaan). Although more than eighty years old, Caleb had no fear. He blessed Israel by trusting God to help him fight and drive out idol worshippers from his portion of land, some of whom were giants (Judges 1:20). Caleb knew that the greater the conflict, the greater the reward. He stood firm to establish the God-given promises and drove out the enemy of Israel.

The Unnamed Man

And the house of Joseph also went up against Bethel, and the LORD was with them. So the house of Joseph sent men to spy out Bethel. And when the spies saw a man coming out of the city, they said to him, "Please show us the entrance to the city, and we will show you mercy." So he showed them the entrance to the city, and they struck the city with the edge of the sword; but they let the man and all his family go. And the man went to the land of the Hittites, built a city, and called its name Luz, which is its name to this day.

Judges 1:22-26

This story takes us to when the House of Joseph was ready to take Bethel from its Canaanite inhabitants. The scriptures tell us about an "unnamed" man in this historical, biblical encounter. Bethel was part of the promised land designated to Jacob's descendants during an encounter with God (Genesis 28:12-19).

The mysterious man exited the city, which was probably part of his daily routine. However, confronted by foreign spies with the request for information needed to take the city of Bethel, his life was altered forever. Whether to help the Israelites or not, in exchange for his and his family's safety, was a critical decision. As with Rahab, the reverence for the God of the Israelites and fear of this conquering nation may have persuaded him to cooperate.

The house of Joseph (tribes of Ephraim and Manasseh) treated him well. Not only did he and his family survive, but he also was granted a blessing to establish and then construct a new city, Luz, within the region. Because of the right decision the man made at the right time, the Genesis 12:3 principle became a reality for this unnamed, albeit important, individual.

Ruth

"Why have I found favor in your eyes [...] since I am a foreigner?" (Ruth 2:10).

Ruth chose to identify with the Jewish widow, Naomi, and the Hebrew people, instead of remaining with her own Moabite people. "Entreat me not to leave you [...] Your people shall be my people, and your God, my God" are words often quoted at weddings (Ruth 1:16). But the context here becomes one of the greatest love stories ever told.

Moab was the son of one of the daughters of Lot. After the destruction of Sodom and Gomorrah, Lot and his daughters temporarily lived in a cave—not unusual in ancient times. One evening, Lot's daughters made sure that their father got drunk. He didn't realize what he was doing and committed incest, resulting in both daughters' pregnancies. It was imperative for women to bear children to carry on the family heritage in ancient times. One of the daughters named her child Moab, which means "from my father," or in modern terms, "incest."

Moab, today's modern Jordan, is the country to which a Jewish citizen of Israel, Eli Melech (Naomi's husband), took his family during a drought in Israel. After Eli passed away, his sons, Mahlon and Chilion, who had married Orpah and Ruth, both Moabite girls, also died. This was the final straw for Naomi, who emotionally had enough. She was extremely miserable with grief in the loss of her husband and sons and had no provision for carrying on in that foreign place.

Naomi broke the news to Orpah and Naomi that she would return home to Israel after hearing that Israel had been restored from a lengthy drought. Both girls wept over Naomi's decision; nevertheless, Orpah kissed Naomi and went back to her Moabite gods, disappearing into the dust bins of history.

We never heard about Orpha again until we learn that she eventually married into the family of Goliath, the Philistines, enemies of Israel.[34] She had an opportunity to continue with Naomi but chose former pagan worship. Perhaps she regretted her decision when she heard just how much Ruth had been blessed by through Naomi.

Let's remember that Naomi asked God to bless and deal kindly with both of her daughters-in-law because they had treated her sons in a kind manner (Ruth 1:8). It's as though she said, "Receive the blessing for blessing us!" In ancient times, people did not convert from one religion to another but from one peoplehood to another. Ruth refused to abandon Naomi and chose Naomi's people—and God. Ruth obviously had heard much about the God of Israel. No doubt, Naomi taught the girls about the one true God of Abraham, to keep Shabbat and the laws of Israel.

By the providence of God, Ruth worked the fields of Naomi's kinsman, Boaz, to provide for Naomi. Boaz took notice,

And Boaz answered and said to her, "It has been fully reported to me, all that you have done for your mother-in-law since the death of your husband, and how you have left your father and your mother and the land of your birth, and have come to a people whom you did not know before. The LORD repay your work, and a full reward be given you by the LORD God of Israel, under whose wings you have come for refuge.

Ruth 2:11-12

Because Ruth loved the Jewish people, she became the wife of Boaz. Ruth and Boaz are the great-grandparents of King David and descendants of Jesus. Ruth's life reflects the redeeming grace of God that brought salvation to the whole world.

Johnathan, Saul's Son

And he said to him, "Do not fear, for the hand of Saul my father shall not find you. You shall be king over Israel, and I shall be next to you. Even my father Saul knows that." So the two of them made a covenant before the LORD. And David stayed in the woods, and Jonathan went to his own house.

1 Samuel 23:17-18

Jonathan, Saul's son, clung to David as Ruth did to Naomi with an unconditional love that would not die. He trusted in David's God, as Ruth trusted in Naomi's God. Jonathan took a back seat regarding the succession of his father's kingdom. He was willing to let David reign without competition. I found it a humbling experience to listen to Jonathan's words to David.

He was not jealous of David; he did not try to compete for the kingdom's rule, which could have fallen to him when his father died, but he was willing to take a lower position. Jonathan joined himself to David in a covenant relationship of holy submission to the God of Israel.

When Saul's three sons died in battle, David grieved the loss of his covenant friend and desired to make good on his promise to Jonathan (2 Samuel 9:1). David found the son of Jonathan, Mephibosheth. "I will show you kindness for Jonathan your father's sake and will restore to you all the land of Saul your grandfather; and you shall eat bread at my table continually" (2 Samuel 9:7). Jonathan had helped protect God's appointed king, which gave a blessing for his son.

Abigail

"Please forgive the trespass of your maidservant. For the LORD will certainly make for my lord an enduring house, because my lord fights the battles of the LORD" (1 Samuel 25:28).

Nabal, who lived in Maon, was a harsh and selfish man. He was a very wealthy man with thousands of sheep and goats that he tented in Carmel. His wife was Abigail, a wise, beautiful, and kind woman. David sent his young men in his name to greet Nabal. They greeted him with a blessing of peace and may have said, "*Shalom Aleichem*" (the ancient Middle Eastern greeting for peace upon the man and his home).

David's men had protected Nabal's men during sheep-shearing time. David's men inquired as to whether Nabal would supply food and nourishment as payment. Nabal replied,

> Who is David, and who is the son of Jesse? There are many servants nowadays who break away each one from his master. Shall I then take my bread and my water and my meat that I have killed for my shearers, and give it to men when I do not know where they are from?

> 1 Samuel 25:10-11

Abigail knew right away that David had sent messengers out of the wilderness to greet Nabal and that he berated and reproached David. He had been given his opportunity to bless but turned away from David and his men. Abigail realized that David and his house were fighting the battles of the Lord for His coming kingdom.

Abigail saw the kingdom and Israel's role as everlasting. She wisely took bread, wine, prepared lamb, roasted corn, raisins, and cakes of figs to David and his men. She also blessed David with good counsel. "And blessed is your advice and blessed are you, because you have kept me this day from coming to bloodshed and from avenging myself with my own hand" (1 Samuel 25:33). As she gave her blessing to David and his army, she asked for the blessing of being remembered in the future. Subsequently, the curse of death came upon Nabal. After his death, David married Abigail.

Too often, the church claimed to sing praises unto the God of Israel but cursed the Jewish people. It should never have happened.

> With it we bless our God and Father, and with it we curse men, who have been made in the similitude of God. Out of the same mouth proceed blessing and cursing. My brethren, these things ought not to be so.
>
> James 3:9-10

Abigail reaped the blessing of repenting for the wrong actions done by her husband.

Ittai the Gittite

"Then the king said to Ittai the Gittite, 'Why are you also going with us? Return and remain with the king. For you are a foreigner and also an exile from your own place'" (2 Samuel 15:19).

It is recorded in the second book of Samuel about a foreigner, Ittai the Gittite, who chose to side with David even after David's plea for him to stay behind. It was a time of chaos. Absalom, David's son, planned to overtake his father and claim the kingship for himself. David decided to flee from Absalom instead of fighting his own son face-to-face.

Israel and some of Judah sided with Absalom, but not Ittai:

> Ittai answered the king and said, "As the LORD lives,

and as my lord the king lives, surely in whatever place my lord the king shall be, whether in death or life, even there also your servant will be." So David said to Ittai, "Go, and cross over" [...] and all the people crossed over. The king himself also crossed over the Brook Kidron, and all the people crossed over toward the way of the wilderness.

2 Samuel 15:21-23

This native of the Philistine city, Gath, was determined to go with and take care of David in his trials. Although a stranger and not of the children of Israel, Ittai was more faithful and consistent in his loyalty to the Jewish King, David, than many who were Israelites by birth. His fidelity brought him a position of great trust as the commander of one-third of David's army (2 Samuel 18:2). The faithfulness of Ittai became a channel through which the blessing of God was released. It allowed him and his children safe passage over the brook Kidron to escape the fury of Absalom.

A loyal servant of David, Ittai refused to bring harm to Absalom just as agreed in the presence of the king (2 Samuel 18:5). No more is said about Ittai, but we can assume he remained faithful, for David was brought back from across the Jordan to be reinstated as king in Jerusalem. The promise: "He will raise a flag among the nations and assemble the exiles of Israel. He will gather the scattered people of Judah from the ends of the earth" (Isaiah 11:11, NLT).

Barzillai the Gileadite

"But show kindness to the sons of Barzillai the Gileadite, and let them be among those who eat at your table, for so they came to me when I fled from Absalom your brother" (1 Kings 2:7).

David, in his final moments of life, spoke this instruction regarding Barzillai to Solomon. He recalled the time he fled from Solomon's older brother, Absalom. David found himself at Mahanaim, a town east of the Jordan. The biblical story relates that he and his companions took refuge there after Absalom's disastrous revolt.

Owing to their hurried flight, David and his fugitives were requiring the necessaries of life, especially when there was growling hunger from a lack of food. Apprehensive about the welcome the Gileadites might extend to them, their fears were quickly abated when three of the richest and most influential men in the Gileadite district actually came to their aid.

Barzillai, the Gileadite, was a wealthy man of Rogelim.[35] Along with two other men from Gilead, he brought beds, cups, wheat, barley, honey, butter, sheep—everything needed to gather strength and refresh the spirits. "For they said, 'The people are hungry and weary and thirsty in the wilderness'" (2 Samuel 17:29). Provisions were generously provided.

Soon after David's subsequent return to Jerusalem following Absalom's defeat, Barzillai guided him over the Jordan. David's long-time friend, Barzillai, was eighty years of age, so he declined

David's invitation to come to live in the capital but sent his son, Chimham, instead (2 Samuel 19:31-39). Before his death, King David charged his son, Solomon, to "show kindness to the sons of Barzillai the Gileadite, and let them be among those who eat at your table" (1 Kings 2:7).

Barzillai's loyalty and extreme kindness to King David brought him and his descendants manifold blessings. Solomon may have allotted Chimham, the son of Barzillai, a "habitation," which, according to some scholars, may have been the inn in Bethlehem significant to the birth of Christ.[36] The kindness of Barzillai was a blessing to King David and was rewarded for generations to come.

Hiram, King of Tyre

"Now Hiram king of Tyre sent his servants to Solomon, because he heard that they had anointed him king in place of his father, for Hiram had always loved David" (1 Kings 5:1).

King Hiram of Tyre, a city in the south of Lebanon, had always been friendly with David, Solomon's father. King David was not allowed to build the Lord's House because of the many bloody battles he fought on every side during his reign. However, King Hiram's craftsmen built David's house (2 Samuel 5:11). He was called upon again when the time came for the House of the Lord to be built.

David instructed Solomon of God's plan for building a House for the Lord in Jerusalem. It was in Solomon's lifetime that God brought rest to Israel. There was no concern that anyone would oppose nor attack his kingdom, so building the Temple and developing the kingdom was the focus during Solomon's reign.

Solomon needed Hiram's trained craftsmen in Tyre to hew timber and cut stone since no one in Israel was as skilled in building as the Sidonians. Hiram agreed willingly to help Solomon because of his long-time friendship and loyalty to David: "As you dealt with David my father [...] so deal with me" (2 Chronicles 2:3). He sent his servants to arrive at the Jappa port on Israel's Mediterranean coast in sea raft vessels carrying cedar and fir trees.

Solomon blessed Hiram year by year with wheat, oil, and wine. Along with provision, land was given in the Galilee—twenty cities, which King Hiram rejected (2 Chronicles 8:2). Peace reigned between the two men and their kingdoms. Hiram's builders continued to hew the trees, and others prepared the timber and stones to build the house in Jerusalem. It actually required a force of 70,000 laborers, 80,000 stonecutters in the hills, and 3,600 foremen to bear the burdens of building the house.

King Hiram was not jealous of King Solomon but also helped him develop a naval fleet for trade (1 Kings 9:27). Hiram's kingdom prospered further during Solomon's reign.

Then Hiram, king of Tyre, answered in writing, which he sent to Solomon: Because the LORD loves His people, He has made you king over them. Hiram also said: Blessed be the LORD God of Israel, who made heaven and earth, for He has given King David a wise son, endowed with prudence and understanding, who will build a temple for the LORD and a royal house for himself!

2 Chronicles 2:11-12

The Queen of Sheba

Blessed be the LORD your God, who delighted in you, setting you on the throne of Israel! Because the LORD has loved Israel forever, therefore He made you king, to do justice and righteousness.

1 Kings 10:9

The Queen of Sheba, ruler of the Sabeans, who lived in the southern Arabian Peninsula, was rewarded with more than she brought to King of Israel. The great knowledge and wisdom of King Solomon had covered the earth all the way to her kingdom. "Now when the queen of Sheba heard of the fame of Solomon concerning the name of the LORD, she came to test him with hard questions" (1 Kings 10:1).

The distinguished queen of a not so far away land visited the famed king of the Hebrew. Perhaps all she had heard about this great man was true. With a great cavalcade procession laden with gifts from her land to the king, she made her way to the palace of King Solomon to approach the king to see for herself if what she had heard was true. When she no longer had any unanswered questions in her heart, Ethiopia's brave and courageous queen uttered a blessing regarding the King.

The Queen blessed God's choice of a King for Israel and brought wealth from her nation to him.

> Blessed be the LORD your God, who delighted in you, setting you on His throne to be king for the LORD your God! Because your God has loved Israel, to establish them forever, therefore He made you king over them, to do justice and righteousness.
>
> 2 Chronicles 9:8

The path of blessing was opened to her and her people, as it is to many today if we take the right passage to God's favor. Oh, that more of us, as followers of Jesus, the Messiah, would be brave enough to blaze the trail, as did the Queen of Sheba, in our community and open up new roads of discovery and blessings for our lives.

The generous spirit of a wise woman of royalty guided the queen to bless King Solomon. In return, she was greatly blessed by him, who "gave to the queen of Sheba all she desired, whatever she asked, much more than she had brought to the king" (2 Chronicles 9:12). The law of reciprocity knows no national borders but crosses over any boundaries or frontiers for those who choose to bless.

Elijah and the Widow of Zarephath

Then the word of the LORD came to him, saying, "Arise, go to Zarephath, which belongs to Sidon, and dwell there. See, I have commanded a widow there to provide for you [...] and when he came to the gate of the city, indeed a widow was there gathering sticks. And he called to her and said, "Please bring me a little water in a cup, that I may drink." And as she was going to get it, he called to her and said, "Please bring me a morsel of bread in your hand." So she said, "As the LORD your God lives, I do not have bread, only a handful of flour in a bin, and a little oil in a jar; and see, I am gathering a couple of sticks that I may go in and prepare it for myself and my son, that we may eat it, and die." And Elijah said to her, "Do not fear; go and do as you have said, but make me a small cake from it first, and bring it to me; and afterward make some for yourself and your son. For thus says the LORD God of Israel: The bin of flour shall not be used up, nor shall the jar of oil run dry, until the day the LORD sends rain on the earth." The old woman went away and did according to the word of Elijah, and she and her household ate for many days.

1 Kings 17:8-15

God instructed Elijah, the Tishbite, to leave Israel for the safety of meeting a woman from Zarephath (Sarepta in Luke

4:26) in Sidon (1 Kings 17:9). The word Zarephath means a smelting shop for refining metals. It was a small Phoenician town one mile from the coast between Tyre and Sidon.[37]

The woman would be the vehicle that God would use to sustain Elijah after the brook Cherith dried up and the raven no longer brought meat (1 Kings 17:6). When Elijah was hungry, he said, "Fetch me, I pray thee, a little water in a vessel, that I may drink" and then, "Bring me, I pray thee, a morsel of bread in thine hand" (1 Kings 17:10-11, KJV). Knowing that the only food she had left was in the small jar sitting beside her, Elijah tested her.

It must have taken a real step of faith for such a woman to receive and sustain the Jewish prophet. After all, she was without a husband. Her meager stock of provisions from which to prepare anything to eat was a tiny amount of oil saved for mixing with flour in order to make bread dough. It was not much. She probably silently thought to herself, *When that's gone…it's all gone!* However, when the elderly Jewish prophet inquired about bread for himself, her heart of mercy opened up, and she fixed a small meal for him.

The Zarephath widow unselfishly provided for the needs of a holy but hungry stomach. She then said to him, "I am going to die" (1 Kings 17:12). In the end, she received "a prophet's reward" (Matthew 10:41).

Joy came to the widow and her son. God provided her with sufficient food and saved them both from starvation for a long while. The Sidonian widow received the Jewish prophet and obeyed his word:

> But I tell you truly, many widows were in Israel in the days of Elijah, when the heaven was shut up three years and six months, and there was a great famine throughout all the land; but to none of them was Elijah sent except to Zarephath...to a woman who was a widow.
>
> Luke 4:25-26

Cyrus

> Thus says the LORD to His anointed, To Cyrus, whose right hand I have held—To subdue nations before him And loose the armor of kings, To open before him the double doors, So that the gates will not be shut [...] "For Jacob My servant's sake, And Israel My elect, I have even called you by your name; I have named you, though you have not known Me."
>
> Isaiah 45:1-4

The beautiful account in the Bible of the gentile king touches the heart. Isaiah prophesied regarding Cyrus a full 150 years before he was born. The first thing to notice about the scriptural passage is that

> Cyrus, a non-Israelite king, is called God's anointed, a term previously used only for Jewish leaders. Second,

Cyrus, although called by the God of Israel, doesn't actually know the God of Israel. Instead, like the vast majority of people in the ancient world, he either worshiped different deities in the form of idols or worshiped none at all. In verse 3, the prophet tells us that God will lavish him with tremendous wealth.[38]

As stated by a Torah commentator,

I've given you the key to the treasury of Babylonia—in order for you, Cyrus, to understand that your rise to the pinnacle of power has come about [...] so that the nations of the world will recognize My great name, and that you will be a salvation for the people of Israel.[39]

The gentile king helped save the Jewish people for a cause, which God had in mind for His chosen people. He was like a savior, a bit like Donald Trump was for Israel during his presidential years. An action that pleased many, especially the evangelicals, was that he moved the American Embassy from Tel Aviv to Jerusalem in accordance with the Jerusalem Embassy Act (1995).[40] We do not yet know how this will all turn out with America and Israel, but for the moment, America is standing with Israel, and may it cause other nations to stand with Israel also.

King Cyrus encouraged the Jewish people to return home to their land and rebuild their Temple with partial finances from his own treasury. He went down in history as one of the greatest deliverers for the Jewish people ever born. This positive action in itself is a great blessing. Blessings engulfed his life because of his willingness to help them. Whether a heathen or a believer, the principle of Genesis 12:3 functions equally for all.

The Shunammite Woman

"And she said to her husband, 'Look now, I know that this is a holy man of God, who passes by us regularly'" (2 Kings 4:10).

Elisha, a prophet of the northern Kingdom of Israel during the reign of Joram, Jehu, Jehoahaz, and Joash, had been a student of Elijah. He performed twice the miracles of his predecessor.

Elisha journeyed on foot to Shunem, a city near the Jezreel Valley, south of Mount Gilboa. Here lived a wealthy woman (*ishah gadol*), which could also mean she had great wisdom, who watched Elisha's ministry in the area—his care and miracles.

The woman must have known she refreshed and cared for someone important to God. Along with her husband, she offered Elisha and his servant a small prophet's chamber to rest on their journeys while passing by their home. In those days, investing in a room with furniture and a lamp for a Hebrew prophet would have been a substantial contribution to his frequent visitations.

One day Elisha asked his servant Gehazi to call the Shunammite woman. She came and stood before him. He asked her how he could repay the kindness shown (2 Kings 4:13). When Gehazi let it be known to Elisha that she was barren and without children, Elisha told the Shunammite woman that she would have a child. It happened just as he said. Her kindness brought a new life into their empty home.

Then he said,

> "About this time next year, you shall embrace a son." And she said, "No, my lord. Man of God, do not lie to your maidservant!" But the woman conceived, and bore a son when the appointed time had come, of which Elisha had told her.
>
> 2 Kings 16-17

Some time passed when Elisha warned the woman of a seven-year famine (2 Kings 8:1). She journeyed with her household to the land of the Philistines for seven years. Afterward, she returned to her land in Shunem but found that it had been taken from her (8:3). The Bible does not explain why, only that an appeal to the king was necessary.

The providence of God would have it that King Jehoram was speaking to Gehazi about the miracles and doings of Elisha. He listened with interest as Gehazi told how Elisha had restored the dead to life. As Gehazi was speaking, the woman and her son entered the king's court. "Gehazi said, 'My lord, O king, here is the woman, and here is her son whom Elisha restored to life'" (2 Kings 8:5). The king restored her house and land, all that belonged to them as well as the fruits of the field from the day she left her fields (2 Kings 8:6).

This Shunammite woman who had reached out in a time of need to an old Jewish prophet received the "double blessing" for her kindness. She bore a son in her old age. When a sudden sickness struck so that the child died, she received him back alive by acting in faith. When her property was taken in famine, she received it back with interest. She reaped the blessings she had sown. Investment in God's work will bring His favor into our own lives.

Ebed-Melech, Servant of the King

Now Ebed-Melech the Ethiopian, one of the eunuchs, who was in the king's house, heard that they had put Jeremiah in the dungeon [...] Then the king commanded Ebed-Melech the Ethiopian, saying, "Take from here thirty men with you and lift Jeremiah the prophet out of the dungeon before he dies." So Ebed-Melech took the men with him and went into the house of the king under the treasury, and took from there old clothes and old rags, and let them down by ropes into the dungeon to Jeremiah.

Jeremiah 38:7, 10-11

Ebed-Melech, an Ethiopian eunuch who worked for the king, took men with him and entered the house of the king. Ebed-Melech was troubled at Jeremiah's treatment for giving the word of the Lord. Jeremiah repeatedly warned, "This city shall surely be given into the hand of the army of the king of

Babylon." His warning included Judah's surrender so that the people may live. It was not a favored message. The officials wanted nothing more than to put Jeremiah to death (Jeremiah 38:4). They cast him into the dungeon (or cistern) of the king's son, Malchiah, which was in the court of the guard.

Then, the Ethiopian eunuch learned about the evil against the Jewish prophet Jeremiah. Jeremiah had been left to starve to death in a cold, dirty dungeon. King Zedekiah listened and instructed Ebed-Melech to "Take thirty men with you from here, and lift Jeremiah the prophet out of the cistern before he dies" (Jeremiah 38:10, ESV). Ebed-Melech took old clothes, rags, tied them together, and let them down as ropes into the dungeon to Jeremiah. He was rescued from the pit but remained a prisoner in the court of the guard.

A king's servant from Ethiopia believed in Israel's God and interceded for God's prophet. He saved Jeremiah's life by rescuing him from a dungeon, which could have resulted in his own imprisonment. God used the "servant of the king," the meaning of *Ebed-Melech,* to preserve His Word to King Zedekiah and the people of Judah. Even though neither the king nor the people listened, and punishment came as a result of disobedience, God protected and blessed the Ethiopian eunuch by sparing his life when Jerusalem was captured and burned. Deliverance came because of his bravery on behalf of the Jewish prophet. The Ethiopian's merciful act delivered Jeremiah from the claws of death.

The Genesis 12:3 principle was at work for an ordinary servant with a heart of compassion. God watches from His throne all the moves of mankind and records deeds of kindness to His people. He knows those who bless and those who curse them. Those who help protect God's message and messenger will themselves be protected.

Cornelius

"Cornelius, your prayer has been heard, and your alms are remembered in the sight of God" (Acts 10:31).

A God-fearing Caesarean named Cornelius, who was working as a Roman army officer, was acquainted with the Jewish Scriptures (the Torah). Scholars believe he most likely was the first gentile to convert to Christianity. Through his conversion, the door of faith opened to the non-Jewish world. His incredible benevolence to the Jewish people, prayerfulness, obedience, and spiritual receptivity characterized this godly Roman centurion.

One afternoon around 3 p.m., he clearly saw in a vision an angel of God saying to him, "'Cornelius!' And when he observed him, he was afraid, and said, 'What is it, lord?' So he said to him, 'Your prayers and your alms have come up for a memorial before God'" (Acts 10:4). God had seen Cornelius's Jewish heart, how he loved and treated the Jews, helped the Jewish poor, and prayed the Jewish prayers right along with them during the afternoon Temple sacrifices.

God prepared Peter to accept the invitation of the worthy gentile. A vision came to him to kill and eat things considered unclean by Jewish law. Three times the message was repeated (Acts 10:16). As Peter pondered the vision, Cornelius's men approached Simon the Tanner's house and asked for Peter by name.

Peter went down and said to the men,

> "You were looking for me? Here I am. What brings you here?" They answered, "Cornelius. He's a Roman army officer, an upright man and a God-fearer, a man highly regarded by the whole Jewish nation; and he was told by a holy angel to have you come to his house and listen to what you have to say."
>
> Acts 10:21-22

The next day, Peter and some of the brothers from Joppa went with him to Caesarea. Cornelius had a house full of friends and relatives expecting great things from the Lord through Peter. Cornelius was the first gentile Peter had accepted as worthy of the Lord's blessings.

> So Peter opened his mouth and said: "Truly I understand that God shows no partiality, but in every nation anyone who fears him and does what is right is acceptable to him. As for the word that he sent to Israel, preaching good news of peace through Jesus Christ (he is Lord of all) [...] To him all the prophets bear witness

that everyone who believes in him receives forgiveness of sins through his name."

Acts 10: 34-43 (ESV)

While Peter was speaking, the Holy Spirit fell on all who heard the word. It amazed the Jewish believers because "the gift of the Holy Spirit was poured out even on the Gentiles" (Acts 10:45, ESV). God chose Cornelius to be the first gentile to receive the outpouring of the Holy Spirit, like the Jewish believers experienced on the day of Pentecost (Acts 2).

We can read about another occasion when Jewish elders came to Jesus and begged Him to heal a servant of another Roman officer. The centurion of Luke, chapter seven, had befriended the Jews. His servant was very ill and ready to die. When the Jewish elders arrived, they implored Jesus instantly, telling Him that the centurion's servant was worthy to be healed because his master loved the Jewish nation, which had been so clearly seen and understood through demonstration. They related to Him that "he loves our nation, and has built us a synagogue" (Luke 7:5).

Jesus went with them as they directed his steps to the Roman centurion's home, where the servant lay. The Jewish elders had responded positively to the servant who was ill because they had seen his Roman master's love being demonstrated to the Jewish nation. They knew Jesus would command the blessing of health upon the sick servant.

Both centurions openly supported the Jewish community

in ways that caused God and man to take notice. What we see here is the ancient principle taking hold—the decree of God in the calling of Abraham, when He promised that "I will bless those who bless you" (Genesis 12:3).

The two gentile centurions may not have known the full impact of what they were doing in blessing the Jewish people, but God saw it and was moved to bless them in return. They practiced the principle of mercy and kindness in blessing the Jewish community. In return, the blessing came not only with the healing of the sick but in the power of the Holy Spirit. God shows no partiality and blesses those who participate in the word he sent to Israel.

Priscilla and Aquila

Paul departed from Athens and went to Corinth. And he found a certain Jew named Aquila, born in Pontus, who had recently come from Italy with his wife Priscilla (because Claudius had commanded all the Jews to depart from Rome); and he came to them.

Acts 18:1-2

The apostle Paul (Shaul, a Jew) asked the congregations to greet Priscilla and Aquilla, tentmakers from Italy. They were coworkers with him in the Lord. He recommends them wholeheartedly. He sojourned with them in Corinth, where he remained in much danger (Acts 18: 12, 17).

Aquila and Priscilla's care for him was met with much gratitude: "who risked their own necks for my life, to whom not only I give thanks, but also all the churches of the Gentiles" (Romans 16:4). Paul and the gentile churches recognized their care for the preservation of his life. In turn, he praised them publicly and honored them by introducing them to the congregations to be warmly received.

Even though they were of the Jewish race, they were part of taking the Gospel to the gentiles and had a church in their own home (Romans 16:5). Their part in discipleship was of great service to the new believers in Jesus. Blessings will never cease from operating in the lives of those who unselfishly give of themselves to help a Jewish ambassador for the Messiah.

Phoebe

"I commend to you Phoebe our sister, who is a servant of the church in Cenchrea" (Romans 16:1).

Paul describes Phoebe as a gentile sister in the Lord. She served his congregation at Cenchrea, a seaport of Corinth on the eastern side of the Isthmus, a passage connecting to larger points. "Her name meant pure or radiant as the moon. She is identified as a woman who wore the badge of kindness."[41] As a devout follower of Christ, she had helped Paul, and others, in a manner worthy of the saints (Romans 16:1-2).

She must have been a woman of some means from the fact that she had planned a long journey to Rome on a business of her own and offered to convey Paul's letter to the saints there. The significance of her visit is implied by the appeal of Paul to the Romans to assist her in whatever matter she required.

Phoebe sowed kindness and acts of caring deeds to Paul. In turn, he blessed her by giving her an excellent recommendation to the congregations. Consequently, they received her well, with open arms after her arrival. Phoebe's blessing of service to Paul, a Jewish apostle, earned her a reputation of kindness and compassion that would carry her name through the ages.

While I have not found all of the silver threads spun in the heart of many accounts of blessing and cursing the Jews throughout the Bible, I am certain there are more strands braided into the beauty of God's Word. I hope that you, the reader, will find more and realize how God blesses those who help guard the apple of His eye. May the examples clearly given us be a blessing in themselves, to all who study and take them to heart.

May we also consider blessing the place God chose for His name, Jerusalem, and the people to whom He chose to bring forth the Word about Messiah to the world. In every historical account of non-Jews touching the "apple of God's Eye" (Deuteronomy 32:10; Zechariah 2:8) that I have given, in one way or another, the contributory benefactor was subsequently favored and blessed by the Almighty. Isn't it wonderful that God has put this blessing woven into His Word for the benefit of mankind so that they would know the benediction upon their lives was similar to the priestly blessing given to the people in Numbers 6:24 (KJV):

> The LORD bless thee [and He did] and keep thee [and He carried it out]: The lord make His Face shine upon thee [and He brought the blessing to them], and be gracious unto thee: [and He discharged grace]: The LORD lift up His countenance upon thee [and He engineered His Glory over them], and give thee peace [He brought about the outcome of their blessing].

My heart burns with passion to see the gentile Christian-church world realize what they have missed, forsake neglecting God's chosen people, and realize that God has plans and purposes for them in the coming Messianic kingdom to this earth. Aside from all the promises yet to be fulfilled in the coming years, Jerusalem is destined to become "the throne of the Lord" (Jeremiah 3:17). Going with Israel is going with God!

A Great Debt

It pleased them indeed, and they are their debtors. For if the Gentiles have been partakers of their spiritual things, their duty is also to minister to them in material things.

Romans 15:27

In the Bible, the Genesis 12:3 principle is a beautiful prototype designed by God and a wonderful opportunity for a blessing to all mankind. It was His doing that the principle was placed in the introductory chapters of the book of Genesis (*Bereshit* in Hebrew). It appears He wanted to make a statement to the world right at the start, and He built His Word around it. One regrettable truth is that most of mankind has chosen not to partake of the offering made by God.

The Almighty's voice of promise still echoes from Genesis to Malachi and, again, from Matthew to the Book of Revelation, i.e., the entire Bible. As long as the earth remains, the principle will continue to resound with its unbreakable connection to a cup of blessing for all who are willing to drink from it.

Down through the centuries and up until today, during their weekly Sabbath meal, Jewish fathers pray for their sons to be blessed as Manasseh and Ephraim (Joseph's sons), and their daughters to be like Sara, Rebecca, Rachel, and Leah. In the Jewish world, the power of a blessing spoken over family and friends takes a prominent place in individual lives. As

Christians, we need to learn the virtues of both being a blessing and receiving a blessing.

Years ago, my husband and I were greatly blessed to have graduated from Christ For the Nations Institute in Dallas, Texas. It is a center for training the revivalists and emissaries of God for the future. At this Bible college, the whole Bible is taught, and the Israeli flag is flown from a campus dormitory balcony for all who pass by the campus on the nearby interstate highway. In most halls of Christian education, replacement theology still reigns supreme but not so at Christ for the Nations (CFNI.org). Blessing the Jewish people was part of Gordon and Freda Lindsay's (its founders) original vision for the Christian campus. As a result, the college has acquired a great reputation for standing with Israel, and God has poured out His blessings upon them for their obedience.

We understood that God spoke through the Hebrews who wrote down his Law and Statutes and that those scriptures are vital today. In the Jewish Scriptures, in what we termed the "Old" Testament, prophets foretold the Messiah's coming. A Jewish womb carried the Messiah to full birth. Jewish people were the first to receive Him as their Messiah. Jewish laborers left their families and livelihoods to follow Him. Jewish multitudes were the first to believe in Him and be healed. A Jewish man gave Him a proper tomb for a Jewish burial, and Jewish people were the first eyewitnesses to His resurrection. Jewish apostles and disciples risked their lives to take the message of His kingdom to the world. The fact is that all the psalmists, prophets, apostles, and, of course, Jesus Himself, were Jewish.

As His Jewish disciples were sent into all nations to spread His message, they died cruel deaths. Information from the New Testament, apocryphal texts, early Christian historians, and oral records passed down through the centuries confirm that all the Jewish apostles died by the hand of cruel oppressors, but they were all faithful to the Lord.

Derek Prince once said, "Without the Jews, we would have no patriarchs, no prophets, no apostles, no Bible—and no Savior! Deprived of all these, how much salvation would we have left to us? None!"[42] Let us always remember his words, words of a great Bible scholar and good friend whom we were privileged to know. His words still echo in our ears today: "We owe a great debt to the Jews."[43]

As we think about the impact of that statement, let us acknowledge that it was a Jewish psalmist who penned many of the lyrics from which the hymns of the early church were written. Many modern worship songs of today are inspired by the Hebrew writers.

According to Patrick Kiger, a researcher with National Geographic, we learn that the Jewish disciples paid a great price to take the message of God's grace to the world. Simon Peter (his real name, changed by the church, was Shimon Kefa) was martyred by the Romans, as were the other Jewish disciples. Historians reported that Peter asked to be crucified upside down so that his death would not be in the same way as the death of Jesus on the cross. And yet, the church historically claims that all Israel rejected Jesus.

Andrew (Andreas), according to Dorman Newman, a fifteenth-century religious historian, received the full treatment when not agreeing to forsake Christ. Andrew was scourged and tied, rather than nailed, to a cross so that he would suffer for a longer time before dying. It is said that he lived for two days, and like His Master, he taught those who passed by him. James (Yaacov), the son of Zebedee (Zavdai), was killed by the sword and beheaded (Acts 12:1-2). John (Johanan) did not die a violent death but passed away peacefully on the island of Patmos from old age.

Philip (Fillipos) made it to Asia and eventually traveled to Heliopolis in Egypt, where he was scourged, imprisoned, and crucified. Bartholomew (Bar-Talmai, son of Ptolemy) supposedly preached in several countries, including India. In one account, "impatient idolaters" beat Bartholomew and then crucified him. In another account, he was skinned alive and then beheaded. Thomas (Tau'ma) preached the gospel in Greece and India, where he angered local religious authorities, who martyred him by running him through with a spear. Matthew (Mattityahu), according to legend, was martyred in Ethiopia, where he was stabbed in the back by a swordsman sent by King Hertacus. According to John Foxe, an English Puritan preacher, James (Yaacov, the son of Alphaeus) was beaten and stoned by persecutors at the age of ninety-four and then killed by being hit in the head with a club. Thaddaeus (Judas or Jehuda/Jude) was crucified at Edessa (the name of cities in both Turkey and Greece) in AD 72. Simon (Shimon, the Canaanite) preached in Mauritania on the west coast of Africa and then went to England, where he was crucified in AD 74.

Whoever wrongly touched these Jewish men before they died broke the command of God, "Do not touch My anointed ones, and do My prophets no harm" (1 Chronicles 16:22). We know that these Jewish holy men did everything they could to take the gospel of the Jewish Messiah to the gentiles (non-Jews).

Today there are multitudes of Jesus followers because of the faithful service of Jews to both God and man. Their work opened up the way for gentiles to worship the God of Israel and know Him as the one true God. Although little was taught about God in the nations, Christians have always proclaimed God as one God, a world without end.

Even though accounts differ slightly from researcher to researcher, early Jewish followers sacrificed their lives in horrendous ways to take the Gospel of grace to the nations that Yeshua died, not only for Israel but also for the non-Jews. These Jewish men did the will of God for the nations. Should we do any less in return? "Doing the will of God from the heart, with goodwill doing service, as to the Lord, and not to men, knowing that whatever good anyone does, he will receive the same from the Lord" (Ephesians 6:6-8).

Going to the hurting and lonely was such a privilege.

While living in Illinois in the 1970s, I had a vision that I will never forget. Two words came to me: "healing balm." We have all heard the phrase "healing ointment" before, but, at the time, I didn't know what was meant by "balm." I now believe it refers to that which was always supposed to be the vocation of the church. Using God's healing medicine, the ointment of divine compassion, mercy, and a love so deep that it is the remedy for restoring the hearts of the wounded from the mistakes of history.

Christian Friends of Israel has sent outreach healing teams to more than fifty cities in Israel over the years because the wounded branches need special care. As Christians, we are devoted to God first through Jesus and then to Jerusalem and the Jewish people. I remember hearing Derek Prince say that the white linen of the bride is the righteous deeds of the saints. Our motivation is to do what should have always been done—to care for the Jewish people. "Owe no one anything except to love one another, for he who loves another has fulfilled the law" (Romans 13:8).

Years ago, in 1980, one of the first survivors of the Nazi occupation I had ever worked with said to me, "I was under Nazi occupation for four years. I lost my entire family and then asked myself, 'Why?'" She continued, "Why did this happen to my people? You were the first Christians to come to me. You were the first Christians to visit my people. You love them, and you hugged them. You have changed my heart toward your people!"

In her opinion, it was impossible for a Christian to reach out to others, to hug, to love, to serve, and to be merciful. She went on to say, "You have changed me. My whole life has changed. I have faith again in Christian people." In other words, she said, "You provoke us to change our mindset."

The Savior's love is unconditional. The Bible says love is the fullness of the Torah and does not harm anyone. Accordingly, divine love is not only the fullness of the Torah, but it is the fullness of Messiah Jesus and all of His teachings. The Book of Romans teaches us that love is unconditional and knows no boundaries.

Our beloved rabbi Yaacov Youlis, who worked alongside us for over eighteen years, once said to me, "During the Gulf War, when the rockets flew around about us, I wrote something about you, Christians, in my diary." I asked him, "What did you write?" He replied, "Only two words."

I asked again, "Well, what were those two words?" He said, "They stayed." What he meant was, "You did not run away when my people were attacked."

It is true that Christianity sadly abused the name of God throughout history. He gave us an order to be the salt of the earth. It might sound a bit strange, but once, someone said to me, "Sharon, I love you so much that I can taste the salt of your tears when you cry." We have to learn to taste the salt of the tears of the Jewish people, for what other people on the face of the earth are so hated by so many people? And for what reason?

In 1985, our Jewish neighbors, Eli and Pnina, invited us one evening for a Sabbath dinner. Then, they asked us why we came to live in Israel. We said, "God told us to, so we sold everything and came to Israel." We continued to give the story of our leaving our families, friends, and all of our possessions to come to Israel because God had directed us to do so. Pnina put her hands in front of her face and said, "I am so jealous of your faith that you would do what God told you to do."

In the 1990s, CFI conducted mercy missions to the Former Soviet Union (FSU), and I led several teams in the search for elderly Jewish survivors in Minsk, Belarus, and Kirovograd, Ukraine, in order to help those hidden away in their modest apartments for fear of antisemites in their neighborhoods. We cooperated with the local Jewish community centers, and I hope to write my next book, "I Sat with the Dry Bones," based upon their stories. I have to mention that I have never seen miracles like what happened in these dark places.

Most of the survivors we found had never told about the horrors of their lives to anyone since WWII and after their return back to their hometowns. We went to them and told them all about Israel and their homeland, encouraged them to come to Israel, gave them gifts of love and friendship, and they told us their personal stories, all recorded in a special book which I have in Jerusalem. "But this is a people robbed and spoiled; they are all of them snared in holes, and they are hid in prison houses; they are for a prey, and none delivereth; for a spoil, and none saith, Restore" (Isaiah 42:22, KJV).

God gave us the assurance He was going before us, past the KGB who followed us everywhere we went, through the scrutiny of airport securities, out of the sight of those who followed us, and even gave us a hard-nosed Chernobyl fighter to hear his story of pain and suffering from the nuclear reactor that blew up on April 26, 1986.

I will go before you and will level the mountains; I will break down gates of bronze and cut through bars of iron.
I will give you the treasures of darkness, riches stored in

secret places, so that you may know that I am the LORD, the God of Israel, who summons you by name.

Isaiah 45:3

From the time we touched down in the FSU, miracles began to happen, the Lord was clearly seen to be guiding us, and more adventures than one can imagine began to transpire. More in my forthcoming book.

I saw many Jewish hearts healed and depression lifted because of our visits. Mercy and kindness went with us. Our experiences were priceless. We just carried God's love and compassion for His wounded people, who were still wounded and surrounded by antisemites. I will speak about this to give evidence of what I've seen, where I went, how they responded, what God did, and how our unreserved kindness lifted their spirits and changed hearts by applying God's healing balm. I am testifying to what I actually witnessed and heard.

The last living witnesses of the Holocaust, whom we visited, suffered much persecution during and after the Holocaust. Some said to us, "You are the first to come and help us work through our pain." Some inquired, "Where have you been all my life?" They had been totally forgotten. We had the cure: unconditional love. We did not ask for anything, we just sat and listened, and the Lord always showed up in some way. They had been remembered. They had come in contact with people who cared. Their depression was clearly so visible when the doors opened, but soon smiles and laughter came and "Please come again!" When we left, the waving of goodbye at their windows until they could see us no more was enough joy and eternal recollections to last a lifetime. This was one of the most memorable moments of our lives.

How can I forget Luba? She was dressed in black when we arrived. She had dressed only in black since the end of the war. When we met her, she said, "How can I speak? I can't cry. Maybe I'm made of stone." In her eyes, we could see how she was suddenly back in the concentration camp, in the middle of the war.

She said, "When I was in the ghetto, they stacked our people like logs." A large tear formed, but it didn't fall until one of our team members started crying. As we cried, Luba sobbed. "Your tears have come to my heart." We watched Luba transform from a stone into a candle.

On the last day of our assignment from God, we were saying goodbye to everyone at a going-away celebration we organized. When Luba walked down the driveway to the little village home, she was wearing a lavender shirt. She said, "I will never wear black again...because you came!" We encouraged her as she proclaimed, "I now know that God exists because you came." She had been healed of her hurt.

Mira was ninety years old and had spent three years in Auschwitz. She had a prisoner number on her arm, which she wanted to show us; however, even as a survivor, she had never received any compensation. She told us as we intently listened, "They [the Nazis] made us eat grass like cows."

We had brought with us food, medicine, financial aid, and a blanket hand-sewn by blind Christians from England. When we gave her the blanket, she said, "Oh, for my suffering!" She clung to her new blanket made by Christians and told us, "I will take this to my grave with me." In her heart, she was seeing that the blanket given in love was some kind of recompense for her pain and suffering, something to hold onto to confirm to her that she was loved by God.

Gersch was a man who had suffered more than anyone we had met. Upon our arrival at his little apartment, he was standing at the window looking aimlessly into the sky. He had lost his wife and children in the Holocaust. After the war, he returned to Belarus, married a second time, and had a new family, including two sons. One day, while he and his wife were shopping for food in the local marketplace, his "neighbors" knocked on the door of his home. It was the last time he ever saw his children alive as they were senselessly and brutally murdered. He was just staring into the dark sky when we arrived.

He was in a deep state of sorrow and despondency. After spending considerable time with him and his wife and sitting at the table to share a meager meal together, giving them the gifts we had brought all the way from Israel, we had to say goodbye. It was then he turned to us and said, "Now I believe in God. He sent you to us. You came to us and showed us love that no one has shown us before."

Then there was Mira. Upon our arrival, even in her nineties, she came down the stairs of her apartment, heading right for our taxi, which had just delivered us to her door. Of all of the stories I've heard and recorded, her story touched my heart so deeply. She said, "When the American soldiers came to liberate Auschwitz, they lined the Nazi soldiers up against a wall. The Americans gave us, survivors, bread for many were hungry. I looked over at the Nazi soldiers, and I saw one that looked so hungry...and I gave him my bread." There was no attitude of self-satisfaction in her story at all, only a humble heart letting us know that she had done actually what Jesus had instructed all of us to do: "love your enemies" (Matthew 5:44).

Many Christian forefathers loathed the Jewish people and taught their congregations to do the same.[44] If only some of our leaders showed the love of God, which Mira displayed to her oppressors, the Nazis, we would have a different world. I often think that we do not really know the height, width, depth, and breadth of the Father's love. We have yet so much to learn.

There were many inquisitions across Europe intended to identify heretics, a crime punishable by death.[45] Spain came to the forefront because of the number of Jews who converted to Catholicism in order to keep their property and position, and for some, their life. Many of those who converted continued their Jewish lifestyle and identity. As their sincerity of conversion came into question, the religious orders took action against them. Hoping to eliminate the problem with the Jewish community, the Edict of Expulsion (1492), issued by Catholic Monarchs Isabella I and Ferdinand II, degreed the order to convert or be expelled.[46] The history of the 300 years of the Spanish Inquisition is complicated and debated. The Catholics argue that the Inquisitions brought order and provided legal systems to save lives.[47] Most history books tell about the countless lives lost and tortured, especially among the Jews.[48]

It is the Holy Spirit that compels people to believe. Yet, the church became vessels of hate, which inflicted pain and horror. It is never right to assume the role of God to judge another and take from them the very process that He works in people's lives.

True, Jewish people are far from perfect, just like the rest of us. The Bible tells us that their sin drove them into exile and that God punished them harshly. The twenty-sixth chapter of Leviticus tells of God's discipline toward the Jewish people. We have seen them suffer. But we cannot forget that God promised restoration: "Yet for all that, when they are in the land of their enemies, I will not cast them away, nor shall I abhor them, to utterly destroy them and break My covenant with them; for I am the LORD their God" (Leviticus 26:44). Through the centuries, there has always been a remnant of the people who feared God and kept the Torah as sacred.

The principle in Genesis 12:3 is not so anyone will worship Israel as a people nor idolize them. But, as a Christian, when you read a Jewish Bible, love a Jewish Messiah, and read the words of the prophets and apostles, all of whom were Jewish, I believe all of us have the task of representing God's faithful love in the way we always should have and to remember that the God of Israel is a covenant-keeping God. Following the commandment of Genesis 12:3 is wisdom.

If Jewish people do not respond to your love, which you show them at first, please wait, as they are testing you to see if they can trust you. They have every right to do so after two thousand years of mistrust and betrayal by "church" people. We must be a blessing in order to remove the curse we invoked upon Christendom, and then only can we be His true witnesses that have backbone about what we believe. We love the Jewish people and pray for them. We will stand on God's side so that He can accomplish His work.

A devout gentile from Hungary once said, "I know that on Judgment Day I will not be asked the same question that God asked Cain after he killed his brother: 'Where were you when your brother's blood called to Me?'" We could rephrase this question as "Why didn't Christians help us?" We do not want the church's past to be a millstone around its neck, holding back the Spirit of God. Did the Good Samaritan hand the injured man a tract (Luke 10:25-37)? No, he knelt down and served the person in need of healing. It could be that one day God will ask you the question, "My people needed someone to lean on. Were you there?"

The congregations in Luther's time were encouraged to look the other way if there was a desperate need for help among the Jewish people around them. "Whoever has a desire to lodge, nurse and honor [...] the worst enemies of Christ [...] with deeds of mercy, Christ will reward him on Judgement day [...] (with) eternal hell and fire."[49] When the Jews rejected Luther's appeal to repent for killing Christ and become Christians, he began to hate. Then, he encouraged pastors to do the same.[50] That hatred would be acted out century after century until finally embraced by the Nazis.[51] Why did the Christians do little? It was taught for centuries that they were not to help "children of the devil."[52] This blindness silenced thousands who looked on while six million Jewish people were murdered during the Holocaust. With God's help, many Christians have broken free from that delusion. Now, we teach others how to be set free by discovering the whole plan of God and how He used the Jewish people to accomplish salvation for the world.

May God give us the humility to see that we are the branches, not the root of the tree. In the end, to some degree, and according to Matthew 25:40, God will weigh each nation on the scales of His sense of justice for His people.

Can we rediscover God's long-lost mission for the church? Are we enough in number to rightly change the future for the course of Jewish and Christian history? Those who read this message and understand how our spiritual ancestors brought us to where we are now in regard to Israel will also understand the importance of the repentance we must do as an ecclesia, a called-out people. If the church really began to respond to become the true face of our Lord, I believe we would never again have to answer the awkward question, "Why didn't the Christians help us?" Asking forgiveness does not pay the debt we owe, nor can it erase the memory or pain. But, it does free us from God's judgment and makes it possible to obey God's mandate to bless who He blesses.

Repentance and forgiveness are more powerful than hatred and are the arsenal we must employ against our common enemy. We must align properly with God's eternal covenant with Israel clearly stated within the Hebrew Scriptures. The Genesis 12:3 principle plays an important part in our spiritual maturity and our coming into our fullness in the Messiah. We need to declare a blessing over Israel and the people upon whom the Lord commanded the blessing.

> The Gentiles shall come to your light, And kings to the brightness of your rising. Lift up your eyes all around, and see: They all gather together, they come to you; Your sons shall come from afar, And your daughters shall be nursed at your side. Then you shall see and become radiant, And your heart shall swell with joy; Because the abundance of the sea shall be turned to you, The wealth of the Gentiles shall come to you. [...] The sons of foreigners shall build up your walls, And their kings shall minister to you; For in My wrath I struck

you, But in My favor I have had mercy on you. Therefore your gates shall be open continually; They shall not be shut day or night, that men may bring to you the wealth of the Gentiles, And their kings in procession. For the nation and kingdom which will not serve you shall perish, And those nations shall be utterly ruined.

Isaiah 60:3-5, 10-12

The Missing Link

> Even so, you must be exceptionally cautious not to
> become arrogant over the natural branches. But if you do
> become proud, remember that it is not you that gives life
> to the root, but rather it is the root that nourishes you.

Romans 11:18 (HHB)

The church's identity with Israel needs to be reconnected
and the "missing link" secured again. Christianity, the church,
or more commonly known to many of us as the fellowship in
Christ, has been trying to see its way forward without God's
chosen people. They failed to realize the missing link has
weakened us. We have become anemic without the Hebrew
roots of our faith. While many have searched and found the
truth, others, in their spiritual hunger, are still probing to learn
more. Christ is at the center of our hearts, and to put anything
before Him would be wrong. My suggestion is to love what the
Father loves, the "apple of His eye" (Zechariah 2:8) and to obey
the Genesis 12:3 principle: "I will bless those who bless you,
and I will curse him who curses you; And in you all the families
of the earth shall be blessed."

Someone once said, "A bowl of soup changed history." In
Genesis 25:27-34, Jacob fed his brother Esau a stew of lentils
and accepted the birthright blessing of the firstborn in return.
You might consider that Jacob stole the blessing and that the
Jewish people have a monopoly on blessings. However, in the

Genesis 12:3 portion of Scripture, we see God giving gentiles (non-Jews) an opportunity to partake in the cup of blessing.

Gentiles who believe in Jesus actually join the community, or Commonwealth, of redeemed Israel. They do not replace them. "There is one body and one Spirit [...] one God and Father of all, who is above all, and through all, and in you all" (Ephesians 4:4-6). Through our faith in Him, gentiles are no longer "aliens from the Commonwealth of Israel and strangers from the covenants of promise" (Ephesians 2:12). Once we are grafted into Israel's cultivated olive tree, whose cultivation came from learning the Torah, we reconnect to the missing link and strengthen our faith in Jesus.[53]

Salvation is of the Jews

The Book of John tells the story of a Samaritan woman who had an unexpected encounter with Jesus. For her to understand who Jesus was, He felt it was important to tell her that "salvation is of the Jews" (John 4:22). The Jewish people and the monumentally important role they will play in the redemption of the world cannot be repudiated by playing it down. Because of this lack of understanding, many Christians are unable to comprehend the importance of Israel in modern times.

Until the missing link of Christian brotherhood is reattached, the fullness of the church will never be complete. Its abridged form of teaching diminishes the beautiful love story between the Almighty, a chosen people, and the ultimate new humanity that will emerge once Messiah returns to Jerusalem. This revelation has been hidden for centuries.

Think about it: how could we possibly read Jewish Scriptures, believe in Jewish prophets and psalmists, trust in a Jewish Messiah as Savior of our world and not include His people? Christians have been victims of a limited and insufficient Christian education program that excludes our heritage in Israel. "For whatever was written in earlier days was written for our learning, in order that through perseverance and the encouragement of the Scriptures we might obtain hope" (Romans 15:14 HHB).

As we reflect further on why Christianity ended up with a missing link in the chain of faith, we must allow all evidence to be presented for examination. Then, we can come to a conclusion as to what part we should play in repairing the break. As we learn that allegorical interpretation of the Bible caused deception (at least in part), our eyes can be opened to God's truth regarding Israel.

Broken Links

Christians need to begin by asking, "Why do we push away from entering into fullness by ignoring the olive tree from which we grew?" Devastating theological errors developed over the centuries from misunderstood idioms. Words taken out of context, wrong placement of the biblical timeline, and a lack of knowledge of Hebrew (the original language of the

Bible) brought about erroneous teaching from church pulpits. Christians have been served from a menu of ecclesiastical sermons penned by gentiles, raised with a western mindset instead of being served a complete meal and drinking water from the wells of Jacob.

Early followers of Jesus called themselves "The Way." It was an offshoot of Israel's olive tree, which is hardly spoken about from the pulpit. For two thousand years, Christianity has attempted to replace Israel by declaring that Christendom had superseded Israel's role as the chosen people, and what resulted was devastating (Romans 11:24-25).

We need to pull back the curtain of yesteryear and observe what happened in the meeting hall of the first council of Nicaea in AD 325 with Emperor Constantine. The lack of concern and coldness toward the Jews stirred up antisemitism among intolerant, narrow-minded, and biased people. It rubbed salt into their already festering wounds of betrayal. Eliezer (Elie) Wiesel, a Jewish Romanian-born American writer and Holocaust survivor, aptly said, "The opposite of love is not hate, but indifference."[54]

In Luke 15:8-10, there is the story of a woman who lost one of her ten silver coins. She searched diligently for it, and when she found the missing coin, her natural reaction was to celebrate. "She calls her friends and neighbors together, saying 'Rejoice with me, for I have found the piece which I lost!'" (Luke 15:8-10). It was impossible to contain her joy, for that which was precious to her was no longer hidden from sight. The Bible says we are to rejoice with Israel because God's word is being fulfilled, as He said it would: "Rejoice, O Gentiles, with His people" (Romans 15:10). Isaiah 66:10 says it like this: "Rejoice with Jerusalem, And be glad with her, all you who love her; Rejoice for joy with her, all you who mourn for her."

Jesus, of course, had a parallel story to tell us about the kingdom of God. When the church lost sight of Israel, it lost a precious jewel, just like the woman and her silver coin. When we connect the missing link in our faith, which is the chosen people, and put our ear to the ground to listen to God's Word about Israel, we will also have occasion to rejoice because that which was lost was found. In our search for the truth, we need to hit the ball into the court of Private Investigator Sherlock Holmes and do our work to investigate the long-buried missing link.

When the parting of the ways came, the detachment that took place between Judaism and Christianity nearly shattered the link between the synagogue and the meeting place of the church. What used to exist among early Jewish believers of Jesus when they shared the synagogue together became a "We don't go to your synagogue, and you don't come to our meeting place." It was a devastating disengagement. The disconnection that occurred between Judaism and Christianity after the destruction of the Temple caused a wide divergence between the only two surviving sects of Judaism.

It will require a continuing great effort to accomplish the reconnection between our two communities of faith. Amazingly, today sundry Bible-believing Orthodox Jews are connecting with Evangelical Christians by coming together to explore the Hebrew Scriptures and to teach the Scriptures to other believers. In all my years living in Israel, I have never met an Orthodox Jew of any persuasion who wanted a friendship or relationship of any kind with Christians. That is, not until today.

The hand of friendship that many Orthodox Bible-believing scholars have extended is amazing and can only be termed a miracle in which God is directly involved. As of this writing, I do not see any type of reciprocation on the part of the church. Therefore, individuals such as ourselves must continue in our quest for truth, unafraid of working together with our Orthodox Jewish friends, confident that we are doing the right thing.

The truth is that most in the church are afraid they might be drawn away from Jesus by Orthodox Jews and that they might be placing our Christian people under the law. Nothing could be further from the truth. In fact, it is just the opposite. In our wonderful contacts with Bible-believing Jewish men and women, they stick to the meaning of the Hebrew Bible, Tanakh, by giving great insights into the New Testament.

They told us in the beginning that if we wished to pray in the name of Jesus, "Please, feel free to do so." There was no preventing us, as Christians, from ever speaking the name of Jesus or praying in His name. We experienced only brotherhood. Some would say that we shouldn't be unequally yoked (2 Corinthians 2:14). I would answer by asking, "Are we unequally yoked?"

All Bible scholars believe in the same one true God of Israel. While Orthodox Jews have not accepted Jesus, nor do most wish to at this time, they encourage us to remain as we are, which is what the apostle Paul taught in Galatians—for Christians to embrace our redemption through Yeshua.

Sadly, some of our Christian pastors are not solid enough in their faith to learn the wonderful Hebrew meaning behind the words in their Bible. Learning from Hebrew gives a much richer meaning to the whole Bible. It is a link that not only brings fullness to the Gospel but is an anchor for our soul. Jesus said, "Do not even begin to think that I came to destroy the Torah or the Prophets, I did not come with the purpose to cancel them but rather to interpret them properly" (Matthew 5:17, HHB).

I had a disappointing and unpleasant experience of being scolded by a Korean pastor who attended one of our annual conferences in Jerusalem. We had invited a good friend of ours, an Orthodox Jewish Bible scholar, to speak on our platform. After the session was over, the Korean pastor pulled me aside and proceeded to tell me he was offended that we would invite an Orthodox Jew to speak to us, Christians! The conclusion he had reached while listening to our Orthodox friend was, "What can he teach me? I am a Christian. He does not know Jesus;

therefore, he knows nothing. I am offended that you would have him try to teach us!" Of course, I was very troubled by his response.

My observation now, after living in Israel for many years, is that while the Jewish people are, perhaps, calloused toward Jesus, they are not hardened. There are more Jewish people today studying Jesus, writing about Him, holding art exhibits, painting and sculpturing Him, and discussing Him than at any other time in history. The link between us on this point is that they know that Jesus was Jewish.

Many God-fearing and devoted Jewish Bible scholars study the Jewish Scriptures five hours a day. How many Christian pastors do the same? Therefore, how can we have *all* the answers when we can't even read Hebrew, the original language of God's Word.

Orthodox Jews also raise their hands in awesome praise unto the one true God. They cry out in agony over the sins of their people so intensely that they can tear their clothing or wail because of the error of Israel's ways. How many Christians shed tears at our meetings today, as did some of our God-fearing intercessors and preachers of years gone by? These scholars have the knowledge of Hebrew under their belts and know the meaning behind the words. Should we simply be another proud Christian, arrogant and in the hubris of superiority, joining the many Christian antisemites who say, "We are the new Israel. You, Jews, are rejected by God."

My husband and I followed the guidance of Genesis 12:3 and later realized that the principle had already been at work in our lives, but not as supposition or conjecture. It had affected our lives dramatically. The "missing link" had been found, and it was our duty to share it with Christians around the world. We began a worldwide travel ministry and traveled to fifty nations, reconnecting the circle that had been broken in the chain of our two faith communities.

General Shimon Erem (1922–2012) was a great friend of mine and met with me before his passing. I loved to listen to his wisdom. He told me of a time when he spoke at a Catholic University in the United States. As he spoke to the assembly, he said, "I have read the New Testament, and it tells me that Jesus tore down the wall between us, but you put it back up!" Their mouths dropped open. He believed that a new light dawned that day about Jewish–Christian relations throughout history, of which, until that moment, they had known nothing. We need to be right on the heels of reconciliation with the root that supports us. "Remember that you do not support the root, but the root supports you" (Romans 11:18). There is no place for superiority. It was never taught by Jesus. We follow the same God of the Jews, Yahweh, the one true God of Israel. He is the God of Abraham, Isaac, and Jacob. When we bless Israel, we bless the God we love.

Living in Israel for most of my life has transformed and deepened my faith. It has also taught me about a Jewish world I had never known before. It is a responsibility for all Christians to make certain that once we learn to love as Jesus taught us, we will never again allow the chain that binds us together to be broken. We must never separate from Israel again. "Do not let the son of the foreigner who has joined himself to the LORD speak, saying, The LORD has utterly separated me from His people" (Isaiah 56:3).

For those who are engaged in helping Christians reconnect to the link that had been missing in our faith and are working toward the eradication of replacement theology, we need to continue to guard the Jewish people and shield Israel on the wings of prayer. It is in our hands to make certain that the next generation of believers will seek the welfare of the Jewish people and never again allow a disconnection. We cannot change history, but we can change the future and no longer tolerate indifference.

Neighbors

> You shall not take vengeance, nor bear any grudge
> against the children of your people, but you shall love
> your neighbor as yourself: I am the LORD.
>
> Leviticus 19:18

No one needs a yardstick to evaluate a direct contradiction of our faith when we read the Jewish Scriptures, follow the precepts of Jewish prophets and apostles, receive the Jewish message of salvation, embrace our Jewish Messiah (Jesus) and end up being indifferent to the His relatives.

I am not ashamed of the Gospel of Jesus Christ. Still, because of the spiritual damage that the Christian religion did during different periods of history to the name of Jesus in front of the Jewish people's eyes, I feel embarrassed. In the name of the cross, we acted and behaved shamefully toward God's ancient covenant people.

A Jewish friend of mine, Jonathan Feldstein, wrote an article regarding some of his relatives in Kanczuga, Poland. He recalled his great-grandparents and their family members who had been shot, their bodies pushed over into a "hastily dug ditch in the summer of 1942."[55] In the article, Jonathan recalled the book *Hidden* that was much like his family's story.

Then, they saw the other eyes, those of their neighbors, the customers in their shops, the people to whom they had sold a loaf of bread the prior week, those to whom the Jewish merchants had given a good price on chickens and eggs...whole families, with baskets of cheese and bread and homemade wine, little ones scurrying along the fringes of the crowd. "Zyd!" they cried. "Jew! Out with the Jews!" [...]

Then a bullet shattered our little sister's face and she collapsed at Mamche's feet, spraying blood in her new white shoes. Next, Tunia dropped onto Senia, her breath a shallow purr. Even before the third shot was fired, our mother fell on them both, trying to protect what was no longer hers. Beside the gunmen, the onlookers, some of whom had tied handkerchiefs over their noses to stave off the scent, clapped and shouted their approval. A burst of laughter skimmed the crowd.[56]

The church, a religious institution that developed independently of the Lord's assemblies of called-out people, totally wandered off the road of integrity and righteousness for twenty centuries as it drifted into total disconnection from Israel. It seldom responded to the call to bless but instead turned its back on Israel, contrary to God's counsel in Isaiah 56:3.

Jesus taught nothing but unconditional love toward the House of Israel, to which He had been called. He never wrote one word of ecclesiastical doctrine, dogmas, or creeds passed on to Christianity by antisemitic forefathers. What is out there today and has been for centuries is alien to the Lord and Messiah. I am certain He would not have anything to do with wrongdoing toward His people and nation. God's mercy disciplined His people with a promise for full restoration. Jesus cried over Jerusalem, knowing there were harsh times ahead but knew that His Jewish brothers and sisters would be brought back to the promised land and would recognize Him as Messiah on His second return.

His counsel of "love your neighbor" (Matthew 22:36-40; Mark 12:31) was forgotten by gentile "converts" to Christianity and is in absolute contradiction to what Jesus taught from the Torah. Thankfully, theological heresy taught by the church has never changed God's promises. The echo of God's words still reverberates through the corridors of time.

> I will make you a great nation; I will bless you And make your name great; And you shall be a blessing. I will bless those who bless you, And I will curse him who curses you; And in you all the families of the earth shall be blessed.
>
> Genesis 12:2-3

I traveled to Poland several times and realized on the first visit that a few of the people I encountered in Oswiecim (*Auschwitz* in Polish) appeared as if something just was not right with their understanding of the Jews. I wondered as God recorded every moment the people had the opportunity to help the Jewish people or to at least stand up for them! Too many betrayed their Jewish friends and neighbors and then had the audacity to go to church without remorse the next Sunday morning. I love the Polish people as my own relatives came from Poland. A principle is operating for all nations in relation to God's chosen people.

Father Patrick Desbois has dedicated his life to unearthing unmarked Jewish mass graves in Eastern Europe.[57] He has uncovered 1,744 unknown, unmarked execution sites and mass graves—covered secrets of the Holocaust. He spent many years going into the villages that surrounded several concentration camps and talked with those who watched the horrors as their neighbors suddenly disappeared. One by one, they recalled the names. Large burial sites were located as they recalled painful memories of Jewish neighbors who were shot and pushed into these graves. First-hand witnesses, for the first time, faced the unthinkable as they talked with Father Desbois.[58] Numerous villagers shared stories with him as they had assisted the Nazis to round up truckloads of Jews. They served the German soldiers food and brought them a gramophone so they could listen to music.[59] They watched as the Germans shot the Jews and dumped their bodies into pits.[60] Desbois recalls "one woman who said she 'walked across the fallen corpses to flatten them another group of Jews were shot.'"[61] Another woman from the same Polish town said, "We could see the blood bubbling."[62] Yet another described that "when the pit was full, they filled it with a little earth. For three days, the ground moved. Some were still alive."[63] Father Desbois goes on to say he wants "to show that the murder of Jews was publicly known, even celebrated" at the time but had been kept covered for a generation. Recent years have unearthed the graves of these "unthinkable horrors."[64]

It is not surprising that our rabbi Yaacov, an endeared and respected friend to CFI who worked with us over eighteen years when he first came to our door and saw our name, Christian Friends of Israel, said to us, "Christians? Friends of Israel? I didn't know we had any." I believe the Jewish community was looking for much more from those who said they followed Christ and waited for those who would stand up for them. Instead, they were faced with cowards and charlatans who pretended to follow the Messiah Jesus calling themselves "Christians."

Where were the neighbors in Dorchester, Roxbury, and Mallapan during WWII when thriving Jewish communities faced their own pogroms? Terrible prejudices against the Jews were common. Even youths would chase their Jewish neighbors with weapons and beat them. Serious injuries, and some deaths, occurred while the police not only did nothing but also participated. Little has been said, but it's time we face the truth—and remember our sins.[65]

Another sad occasion during WWII was when the International Red Cross, as the world-renowned humanitarian organization came to be known, lost their moral compass. They "failed to protect the Jewish people." No one from the Red Cross protested the Jewish murders that were going on by the Nazis. They chose "silence" just as the Christian neighbors chose silence.[66]

Sharon with Concentration Camp and Ghetto Fighter Association, our first partnership.

Sima Skurkovitch, Bergen Belson Survivor, my constant companion and teacher.

Another true story of my experiences was with a survivor from the Bergen-Belsen concentration camp, Sima, who made a huge impression on my life at the beginning of my private visits to the homes of survivors in the late 1980s. Sima was one of the first survivors to host a Christian in her home during that period of time. She did not hesitate to express her feelings toward me as a Christian.

The first time she met me, I wanted to hug her, but she coldly said, "Don't touch me. Your people pulled down the shades and closed the doors on my people. I don't want anything to do with you. I have lost faith in your people!"

It took years before I had proven that my love was genuine, that true believers in Jesus would never do the things she saw people do toward her people. She came to me one day and said, "I have watched you. You really *do* love my people. You hug them. You love them. You serve them and have changed my heart, given me faith *in your people* again!"

If only Christian neighbors would have pled for their Jewish neighbors! Instead, they spit on them! Where is the shame that Christianity has wronged the Jewish people? Job said, "These ten times have ye reproached me: ye are not ashamed that ye make yourselves strange to me" (Job 19:3). The wrongs remain inside the church still today (Job 19:4).

Multitudes exalted themselves against the Jew. "If indeed ye will magnify yourselves against me and plead against me my reproach" (Job 19:5). The root of the matter is still antisemitism, and the worst kind is Christian. It is the greatest blow Jesus had to take on the cross, I'm sure of it. How it must have cut Him to the core, and God hates it. I wonder if anyone has pondered on Psalm 5:6. People repaid evil to those who were at peace with them.

> If I have repaid evil to him who was at peace with me, or have plundered my enemy without cause, let the enemy pursue me and overtake me; yes, let him trample my life to the earth, and lay my honor in the dust.
>
> Psalm 7:4-5

Martin Luther's instructions to pastors were to teach their congregations to look the other way.[67] "To look the other way" has been passed from generation to generation, thinking that it is a Christian duty. It is tragic. Some nations stood in the gateway for the Jews when they made it to their homeland on the shores of Palestine on worn-out ships. They turned them back to sea, where many drowned within visible distance of the shores they yearned to walk on.

The Bible warned against such actions and the repercussions of such dealings. These nations were warned by God, in advance, through the prophets of Israel and have paid a heavy price. "I am exceedingly angry with the nations at ease; For I was a little angry, And they helped—but with evil intent" (Zechariah 1:15).

Indeed, countless pew warmers in Europe and America's local

churches did not bless—they cursed the Jews. Undoubtedly, "Martin Luther paved the way to the Holocaust."[68] However, much brick and mortar have been used to continue the despicable road that many today insist on traveling. I advise reading the books *And So It Was True* as well as *While Six Million Died.*[69]

To be equitable in my observations, I have to say that there are many names of people engraved on tombstones in Christian cemeteries during WWII who did not have an opportunity to show a Jewish person love and compassion. I rejoice to see that many Christians today join the ranks of repentance for past sins. It is wonderful to see reconciliation taking place as we celebrate together with the Jewish people, the restored homeland, and being connected to our Jewish roots. My beloved people, Christians around the world, are awakening to truth and not ashamed to face it and ask forgiveness and to grab hold of the promises for Israel today. What a huge blessing this is to my heart.

Today, there are approximately 192,000 Holocaust and ghetto survivors still alive in Israel.[70] There were over 350,000 when CFI began to reach out to them in 1986. Our teams reach out to the last living witnesses every day. We share the healing love of God and do our best to meet needs they cannot provide for themselves. We are a safe place for them to come to in time of need, and we represent the Lord Jesus the way it should have always been done—unconditionally.

The Church's Hall of Shame: Lost Moments

That you may remember and be ashamed, and never
open your mouth anymore because of your shame, when
I provide you an atonement for all you have done, says
the Lord GOD.

Ezekiel 16:63

There have been countless missed opportunities that are
gone forever. The time remaining to put the Genesis 12:3
principle into action is known only to God. We should not
rest in our searching for the truth until we have thoroughly
worked through what caused the historical church's chronicled
and inexcusable responses to God's chosen people during their
times of calamity.

It is a painful journey to walk through Christendom's hall of
shame. Every step is one of bewildering disbelief. In the corridor
of Lost Moments, we would have to pause and think, *What if?*
Suppose the heads of neighbors didn't turn away? Imagine for a
moment hands reaching out to Jews who were suffering? How
did such emotional emptiness assume control over people's
consciences at dangerous times for the chosen people? The sin
of indifference reigned with a vengeance. What about the stolen
Jewish goods in Poland, which became Christian property after
the Jewish roundup? The chicken soup on the stove had not
yet turned cold before crosses were nailed to the doorposts of
former Jewish homes!

It clearly can be seen of those who bore fruit and those who displayed rotten fruit. The history books reveal that the church had stumbled when it came to Israel and the key role in world redemption. It is time to research and review how deep our spiritual roots push downward in the soil of the Jewish nation, for the root of the olive tree of Israel supports us, not we the root! (Romans 11:18).

The mark of Cain remains on the walls of both Roman and Greek halls of shame. The hallway was dark and morally disturbing. But, praise God, there were a few shining lights. We praise the name of the Lord for every Christian who obeyed their spiritual and moral convictions. Those who acted upon them firmly held faith and beliefs of protecting the chosen people when faced with a situation in which their brother, Jacob, needed help.

Someone once said, "When all is said and done, the way the majority treated the minority throughout history is without excuse." During the last World War, many "Christians" sided with the Nazis and abandoned their Jewish brothers and sisters through the sin of betrayal. Throughout the ages, paltry Christian assistance during difficult epochal times of life and death for the Jew has been a disgraceful behavior pattern.

Where were Orthodox Christians during large-scale Russian pogroms and antisemitic riots from 1881 until 1902 before WWII that I have spoken so much about? Why are the numbers so small of Jews rescued from death? Why did Christianity lead the Crusades of 1095–1291? Why didn't those belonging to respectable churches protest those mounting their horses with crosses as their weapons, and even worse, crosses engraved on their shields? These campaigners during medieval times blazed a trail through Europe, which ended in the murdering of thousands of Jews who happened to be "in their path!"

Dr. Michael Brown wrote in his very detailed book, *Our Hands Are Stained with Blood*, the tragic story of the church and the Jewish people.[71] Not all Christians hid or turned their backs. Genuine believers in Jesus were also persecuted along with the Jewish people. I had often wondered if the outcome would have been different if all Christian residents of villages throughout Europe would have courageously stepped in front of their Jewish neighbor's door to announce, "If you take our neighbor, you must take us too." Most gentiles held back, hiding behind their doors until Nazi thugs removed the Jews from their homes for deportation.

There were too few heroes like Poppa Ten Boon, Raoul Wallenberg, and Oscar Schindler. Oscar Schindler, a womanizer, alcoholic and worldly businessman, showed more compassion than most complacent people of faith.

One Christian pastor recently stated, "The church is hopelessly antisemitic." My friend, Tommy Waller of HaYovel Ministries, mentioned to me that the church needs to be reminded of the severe criticism of the "holiness and hell-fire-and-brimstone" sermons clergy once delivered to American

Christians. Much like forced conversion, the Holy Spirit does not lead the way during hateful sermons. If anyone feels I am too negative, I only want the truth to come out because I love the church and desire to lead by example.

Healing broken hearts.

I personally helped care for a Holocaust survivor named Grunya, who had survived eight concentration camps. She visited Poland before her death, the place she had lived as a young girl. She had gone to revisit her childhood home, only to have the door slammed in her face when she asked, "May I come in?" She simply wanted to see once more the place she had once called "home."

After she immigrated to Israel, it was my honor to have been a part of her life. She had suffered so much just because she was "Jewish." Before meeting me, she had never before known or felt genuine Christian love from any gentile. When I first gave her a warm hug, I felt like a human being who had turned to stone. I couldn't feel the warmth flowing in her blood. She had been so mistreated, rejected, and hated because she was a "Jewess."

I learned that the Gestapo had brutally beaten her as a teenager. They had stomped on her feet with their big black boots and pulled all of her fingernails off. She was let go, but she saw three women hanging on a rope after walking through her hometown plaza square. She recognized the clothing of one: her mother's!

She said to me, "Do you realize how I felt? I could not cry out, or I would have been shot. Why did they do that to my mother?" I saw the scars from the Nazi dogs who had chewed her legs and saw the deformations on the back of her neck from being tortured.

At the time of the liberation of Auschwitz, where she ended up, the Nazis tried to drown Grunya, but they failed. The Americans liberated the camp. Her life had been one of darkness since she was separated from her parents as a youngster.

On her birthday, God impressed upon my mind that she had never had a birthday party since her childhood home was broken up and parents and children were parted. She was a very young girl when her parents were separated from her by the Nazis. I wondered what we could do to help heal the pain of all the suffering she had endured. I shall never forget the answer that came into my spirit. God impressed upon my mind the words, "Grunya has never had a birthday party!"

The "surprise" event included decorating the kitchen at Christian Friends of Israel with red hearts and balloons, a beautiful birthday cake, and gifts of love. As the door opened to the kitchen where the party was held, a hard and broken Jewish woman whose body still felt like a stone was touched by a wave of Christian love like she had never experienced. The love was all "just for her."

This wounded elderly woman became dearly beloved. Pathetic and apathetic Christian neighbors had crushed her. But on this day, warmth, love, and compassion were written all over each gift, balloon, and card. I do not think that anyone in that room will ever forget the floodgate of her heart, which opened up in full force; the dam of depression and hopelessness broke as the wall holding back the tears crumbled into a million pieces. A Niagara Falls moment took place in her heart. Grunya never knew she could be loved so much!

After that day, she was never the same. Her broken heart began to heal, but the repair work would take much time as we applied the unconditional healing balm of God's love to her life. This healing of a precious Jewish survivor is a beautiful memory permanently impressed in my mind.

Whenever I become reflective of the wonderful years spent ministering to the broken hearts of the returning to the land survivors, all I need to do is hit "rerun" in the computer of my mind. Then, the days spent with Grunya reappear. It was one of those moments that could never be reproduced nor duplicated anywhere in the world.

If only she could have received that kind of love and compassion during the nightmare of time she passed through, I believe her sadness about life would have been so much less. It was my blessing, and the blessings of others who also knew Grunya, to have been a part of her life and bear fruit that was sweet in her life before her passing. It was moments never to be forgotten.

I have been honored to help many Jews find their way back to Jerusalem after many centuries. There have been many roadblocks and obstacles to work through. The Christian journey back to Jerusalem has found plenty of debris as well: spiritual pride, arrogance, apathy, hatred, Christian antisemitism, hypocrisy, and intolerance, to name a few, lay on the holy highway. These are stumbling blocks that have impeded the healing process in Jewish–Christian relations.

Satan makes it his mission to curse who and what God blesses because he hates God and those who carry out His will. We cannot erase the past. The halls of shame darken every society. Therefore, we must no longer hide in denial but allow the Holy Spirit to shine the light of truth. Stand for God's truth and stand with Israel regardless of adversity.

"Pray for the peace of Jerusalem: May they prosper who love you [...] Because of the house of the LORD our God I will seek your good" (Psalm 122:6, 9).

Meeting at the Bridge

For Zion's sake I will not keep silent, for Jerusalem's sake
I will not remain quiet, till her vindication shines out
like the dawn, her salvation like a blazing torch.

Isaiah 62:1

Former Soviet refusenik and prisoner, Israeli politician,
human rights activist, and author Natan Sharansky, was released
from a prison in the Soviet Union. He landed in Israel on February
11, 1986. My husband I had just arrived in Israel, and "refuseniks"
was the buzzword all across Israel at the time. Refuseniks were
Jews whom the Soviet Union would not allow leaving.[72]

At that time, little did we know that we would be called
upon to become a voice in Zion for the Jewish people across
the world. Many former Soviet Union refuseniks immigrated
to Israel in the '90s. These are precious Jews who had hidden
their identity as Jews for several generations. Christian Friends
of Israel became a friend and helped many of them to celebrate
the feasts and to identify with their Jewish heritage. Many have
died in the land that their grandparents spoke quietly about.
God had a set time to wave the banner for the Jewish people to
return home, but it has not been easy for them. Many reached
out to CFI for help through the years who had been doctors,
lawyers, professors, musicians, dancers, etc., but gladly gave up
their careers, income, homes, and possessions after pleading
with their own government to let them go.

171

One similar area of our lives corresponded with Mr. Sharansky: there came a time in our lives when we had to cross a bridge between two worlds. Returning to the great devastation of Jewish lives during World War II (1933–1945), when the Jewish people were despised and rejected everywhere. It was fashionable at one time to call the Jewish people "wandering Jews," and much worse, "dirty Jews."

Rachel Sharansky Danziger, a Jerusalem-born writer, wrote about her father,

> The bridge was Glienicke Bridge, of Steven Spielberg's "Bridge of Spies" fame. When my father walked onto it he was a prisoner in the Soviet block, though a free man in spirit. He found freedom on the day he stopped hiding his opinions. He earned freedom as he fought for his right to be a Jew in Israel, and for his fellow Russians' human rights. He preserved it as the KGB imprisoned his body, trying and failing to force him to recant. After nine years of imprisonment, my father stepped off Glienicke Bridge, and became a free man in body as well.
>
> Every year, on this day, my family gathers for a private "seder" of sorts. My father wears the *kipa* a fellow inmate made for him. He pulls out the little Psalms book that was his companion in prison. And like the children on Pesach, we ask questions to celebrate this exodus. When we were younger, my sister and I mostly

wanted to understand what "prison" was, and were there animals there, perchance? But as we grew and matured, our questions expanded with us. How did you find the strength to go on, Ima and Abba? And how did you survive the shock of normal life, once restored?

A lifetime of questions wrought a curious effect: While I've never seen Glienicke Bridge with my own eyes, and I naturally couldn't see any of the struggle for myself, I feel like I did. Glienicke is ingrained in my blood, in the inner geography of the self. There, right there inside me, it spans over decades and pain. Archipova Street, where my parents first met, is behind it. A little to the side, I can glimpse Vladimir Slepak's Moscow apartment, and the moment of my father's arrest.

Somewhere within me stands a lit room in Rabbi Zvi Yehuda Kook's Jerusalem apartment. It's dark outside, but the rabbi is up. Far, far away, the Soviet authorities are plotting to accuse my father and his comrades in arms of treason and espionage. My mother's mentors, Rabbi Tzvi Tau and his wife Hannah, brought her to talk with Rav Kook. Standing in the little lit room, surrounded by his students, the elderly rabbi screams. "Our brothers in Russia are in danger," he yells. "We must fight for them." Plans are made, and the base of my mother's future struggles is formed, right there in the little room. This group will come to be known as "I am my brother's keeper," the headquarters of a decade-long campaign.

"But Rabbi," exclaims one of the students, "what about learning Torah? Wouldn't this struggle cause *bitul* Torah?" The rav slams his hand on the table. "He who does not know when to close the books," he thunders, "shouldn't open them in the first place."

My inner map breaks into many different alleys at this point. To the left lie the various two-room apartments that hosted the headquarters of the struggle in the following years, right there in people's private homes, between growing children and domestic routines. To the right lie the people who embraced the cause abroad. I can see my mother marching with them, talking with them, asking and accepting their help. I can see her sleeping on countless couches in people's homes from Vancouver to Brussels, from Paris to New York. I can see them embracing her and giving her strength.

Ahead lies a different kind of struggle. Far, far removed from the clamor of demonstrations and phone calls and speeches, my father sits in a cell, fighting a lonely war. "Recant," press his gaolers. "Recant, and you can leave."

But my father isn't truly alone. Despite the distance, despite the quiet, he is tied to the marching masses. He is tied to the Jewish People. He can hear their voices. And he wouldn't let them down.

In recent years, our children started asking the questions. Animals became prominent again, as did the diet in prison and my father's book of Psalms. I watch them walking the same paths we did as children, their eyes wide with wonder as they form their own inner geographies. But first, before the questions begin, we make sure to tell them the basic story: Bad people didn't want Saba to come here, so they locked him in a little room. Savta yelled, "Let Saba come to *Eretz Yisrael*," but they didn't listen to her when she yelled alone. So Savta went all over the world, and because all Israel are responsible for one another, Jews everywhere started yelling with her. They yelled so loud, and for so long, that the bad people had to let Saba, and his fellow Jews in Russia, come home.

As my parents' daughter, I am forever aware that I owe my existence to the people who yelled with my mother. I wouldn't be here today if you, the Jews of the world, wouldn't have opened your hearts and your homes and your purses. You marched in rallies, sent letters to your representatives, paid my mother's tickets as she flew from one demonstration to another. You hosted her. You encouraged her. Your yells broke through the Iron Curtain. They broke into my father's cell long before they broke him out of it. And they broke into my inner geography, where they ring and echo to this day. I want you to know that I remember, and that I am grateful. I want you to know that when I saw my parents playing with their grandchildren near Lefortovo Prison several years ago, it was your victory that made me almost dance with joy.

Thirty-five years earlier, my father's KGB investigator told him that "we don't let heroes leave Lefortovo alive." You, the Jewish People, proved him wrong. Your spirit and strength in those years freed a man, and brought an empire to its knees. When I feel tired, when I fear for the future...I go back to your echos inside me and find hope.[73]

America and Europe today desperately need a reformation. An American pastor has been quoted on the internet, saying to his congregation, "I would rather have you fix my car than to pay for a trip to Israel." Others are writing on the internet that if you love your Hebraic roots and foundations, you are not even a Christian. Conversely, in Africa, Asia, and India, where there is no baggage of replacement theology, the spiritual leadership, as well as congregants, easily accept the Jewish people, and in most places, the cry of their heart is to receive teaching.

Those who were never indoctrinated with replacement theology welcome the opportunity to learn about their Hebraic roots. When European immigrants came to America, part of the possessions they carried was the replacement theology from their churches. Personally, as a Christian, I am indebted to Bible scholars in Israel, both Christian and Jews, who trusted me enough to talk to me about a dreadful and alarming truth.

As stated in a previous chapter, there are a number of churches that have divested from Israel and those that see themselves as Israel's replacement. Some are somewhere in-between and carry a lack of concern for their future as a possible enemy of Israel. Thankfully, there are some who have actually made documented repentance as a denomination.

Ever since the Confessing Church in Germany issued the Barmen Declaration in 1934, Lutherans, both European and American, have struggled with issues surrounding the role of the church during the rise of Nazism and WWII. Most recently, here in the United States, this struggle led in 1994 to the official condemnation by the Evangelical Lutheran Church in America of Luther's 1534 antisemitic pamphlet. Continuing along the path of repentance and reconciliation, the ECLA in April 1998 issued the draft of a document on Lutheran-Jewish relations, requesting comment from academics and clergy associated with the church. A final version was adopted on 16 November 1998.[74]

Our Amish brethren expressed remorse to Israel by breaking all rules of their own creed to board buses and airplanes to make a pilgrimage to Israel to denounce what Christendom did to the Jewish people throughout the centuries. They carried the torch of honesty and reality in regard to the sincere regrets and repentance toward the Jewish people that is due them.[75]

A group of German Protestants has distanced themselves from the antisemitism of its founder, Martin Luther stating, "We cannot ignore this history of guilt."[76] There was a discussion to remove the carving on the façade of the Martin Luther Church in Wittenberg, Germany. However, at the time of this writing, the detestable carving remains.[77]

In the act of reconciliation, the Catholics made an effort to right wrongs done toward Israel. John Paul II repented for errors of his church over the last 2,000 years, citing religious intolerance and injustice toward the Jews and asked forgiveness, the "most sweeping papal apology ever."[78]

Over the years, I saw a greater number of Jews willing to trust Christians, stepping into our world to become friends, and a full-fledged outreach to include us in learning the Torah, the love of their hearts, the language of the Messiah, Jesus. Their biggest concern at the beginning of our relationship building was that they might offend Christians in speaking to them, not knowing the lingo or the language in which church people think.

Jesus would have stopped His *ekklesia* from separating from the Hebrew foundations. Now, not only is Israel being restored, but we are coming back together with the original carriers of the Torah. Many in the Jewish community are accepting the fact that Christians play a role in the restoration and that they have a vital role in taking God's name to the world.

> Rabbi Jacob Emden wrote that "Jesus brought a double goodness to the world. On the one hand he strengthened the Torah of Moses majestically...and not one of our Sages spoke out more emphatically concerning the immutability of the Torah."[79]

It is amazing that after 2,000 years of trespasses in which the organized church wrongly treated the Jewish people, that I found the Jewish people so willing to look beyond the past and want to reach into the future with Christians. I believe it all happened in God's timing and because of the "healing balm" of unconditional love in which so many of us were giving. It paved the way for healing the pain of betrayal. It did not take the pain away, but the trust, which had been totally lost, was restored to a certain degree.

This is progress. Today we have a Bridge Builder's online chat site where we share our thoughts and our deepest concerns about Jewish–Christian relations. Orthodox Jews and committed Christians walk through tough subjects and areas of differences in opinion, but it has to be done...and it is working.

As Christians continue to sort through buried treasure, they will see Jesus in a new light. Many have begun to understand in context why He spoke what He did, why He did what He did, and what He meant when He taught. Since Jesus would have spoken in Hebrew and Aramaic, we, who speak English, must look into "the meanings behind the words" in our Bibles. This is called "exegesis." We must not practice reading into something that may not be there, as this is error.

Many believers are rejoicing in the new biblical Hebrew nuggets found buried for centuries. Since that discovery, the Christian world has opened up to Bible prophecy and how it relates to Israel. The spade that broke the ground of discovery regarding Israel and our Hebraic roots for Christians has now been carried back to the tool shed; however, the Hebrew roots are visible like never before. The ground of the Christian heart lies open to discovering themselves, the spiritual treasures lying among the roots. The rootstock on which we are "grafted in" has been resurrected from the burial ground in which it lay for centuries.

Every true follower of Christ should be able to read these beautiful passages in the books of the New Testament and honor our foundational roots. From my point of view, this is key to standing with Israel and should help anyone take that first step across the bridge of brotherhood and friendship with Israel.

Dr. Geoff Barnard explains Romans 11:11-12 (KJV) so comprehensively and clearly.

> I say then, have they stumbled that they should fall? God forbid: but rather through their fall salvation is come unto the Gentiles, for to provoke them to jealousy. Now if the fall of them be the riches of the world, and

the diminishing of them the riches of the Gentiles; how much more their fullness?

Dr. Barnard compares the New International Version, translated to read as "salvation has come to the Gentiles to make Israel envious."[80] It is so obvious that today's church is trying hard to make Israel envious of what we have, but it has not worked. Today, Israel is anything but envious of the church after centuries of shameful treatment, which happened in Europe when Abraham's descendants needed us. In discussion with me, Dr. Barnard made an interesting conclusion, saying there is a world of difference between *envy* and *jealousy*. In particular, envy is a sin (see Mark 7:21-23; 1 Peter 2:1) and may be defined as wanting something (or someone) that does not belong to you. Another word for envy is covetousness. Envy is breaking the tenth commandment. On the other hand, jealousy is wanting and/or reclaiming something or someone back that actually belongs to you. According to Paul, the gentiles have been saved to provoke the nation of Israel to jealousy. We need to help them reappropriate what belongs to them. Generally speaking, the institutional church has done a very poor job in doing this, with some notable exceptions.

My stance throughout this book is that we need to be in an honorable and proper relationship with Israel, according to the Genesis 12:3 principle. Once we realize we have come into the Commonwealth of Israel through Jesus, the Messiah, we will have joined ourselves to Israel, as did Ruth, the Moabite.

From my standpoint, we should never think of God removing our call to be a part of the Commonwealth of Israel. Instead, as Christians, who have embraced the God of Israel, and Israel's Jewish Messiah, we must remain true to God, the Father, Yeshua the Son, and the Holy Ruach of God (Holy Spirit) but remember He is one God, not three.

There were "multitudes" throughout the land of Israel, in the days of Jesus, who loved Him. The crowds who followed Him were getting so large Scripture tells us they were getting ready to cry out the messianic welcome and crown Him King. This He could not allow happening before His time. First and foremost, and of paramount importance, was that He had to die first, for the sins of *all* people. If the Jewish people had recognized and believed in Him and had gone so far as to place the crown upon His head, at His triumphal entry into Jerusalem, then He would have become the king of the Jews *only*. The world would have known Him to be "Israel's King," and where would that have left all of the non-Jews in the world?

Would they then have to become Jews in order to be redeemed by Israel's King? That would have placed all of the non-Jews in the ancient and modern world in an extremely difficult place. It would have actually placed them outside the kingdom because non-Jews were not even allowed into the Temple at the time of Jesus. During the days of the Temple in Jerusalem, there was a sign that strictly forbade gentiles from going any further than the Court of the Gentiles. If they did, it could mean death.

Because the God of Israel also loved everyone created in His Image, He sent Jesus to tear down the wall between Jew and gentile. My friend, General Shimon Erem, a patriot and decorated hero of Israel, founded Israel Nexus and loved His people and Christians who shared our Judeo-Christian heritage, recounted the story of when he spoke to a Catholic university in the States. He said, "I told the student body that I had read the New Testament, and I saw that Jesus had torn down the wall between Jew and Christian…but that they had helped to put it back up!" Mouths dropped, and eyes rolled. He told them, "You need to learn your Christian history and do all you can to correct it."[81]

If Jesus had been Israel's King alone, we would not have been allowed to come into the Commonwealth of Israel (Ephesians 2:12). Israel had to make a contribution to the death of its Messiah. It was only Israel that had been chosen by God to sacrifice the Lamb. It could not have been the non-Jews even though the non-Jews, the Roman soldiers, undertook the role of His persecutors and thrust upon Him their harassing and oppressive, brutal treatment.

Unconquered by death, Jesus cried with a loud voice of unexhausted strength and delivered up His spirit into the Hands of His Father. No one else ever did this or died in this way. His birth was unique. His life was unique. His death also was unique. In "laying down" His life, His death was differentiated from all other deaths…

Who but a Divine person could have done this? In a mere man it would have been suicide: but in Him it was a proof of His perfection and uniqueness. He died like the Prince of Life![82]

Swords will be beaten into cutting blades of plows. Weapons will be used for cultivating the soil for the furrow. Without weapons, people will have to get along and concentrate on better lives. As believers, we know that only the Prince of Peace, *Sar Shalom*, Yeshua the Lord, can usher in true peace in place of the chaotic and rebellious uprisings taking place in so many places of the earth today.

One of our functions, as His disciples, is to carry out the task with Israel of spreading the knowledge of the God of Israel around the world. It is to be a "voice" for Israel. For the sake of Jerusalem, we cannot remain silent. As a Christian, I believe that His Excellency will be recognized as the greatest of the King of Kings and Kings of Kingdoms globally. Jesus came to show us the way to the Father! The Father is the supreme goal of our faith. His Name will bring blessings to the whole earth during the kingdom's reign. "For the earth will be filled with the knowledge of the glory of the LORD as the waters cover the sea" (Habakkuk 2:14, ESV). When the roll call of nations occurs, we want to be standing in a position where we know we have served the Lord through blessing His Brethren and not cursing them. "Blessed is the nation whose God is the LORD; and the people whom He hath chosen for His own inheritance" (Psalm 33:12, KJV).

There are many individuals and congregations who have asked forgiveness, but perhaps it would bring greater good and perchance come a worldwide cleansing of the Christian church and a better chance for revival to occur during our lifetime. We need to return to early Christianity's message of "we are still a part of Israel." Meeting in the synagogues, studying the Torah, and celebrating the Jewish festivals and Shabbat faded away. The spiritual dryness in so many of today's modern churches, I believe, very well could be a partial result of never renouncing replacement theology. The "going it alone" without Israel has left a spiritual vacuum that cannot be replaced by other things.

By God's mercy and grace, the Custodian of our salvation graciously visited many in the evangelical world who were open to God's Word on Israel. Both communities of faith began walking across the bridge of courage to meet one another. Hearts on both sides were open, and today, we have a large contingency of both "them and us" walking across the bridge to get a better view of Israel's side. Israelis are also traveling to the nations to meet with Christians in their environments and are willing to speak in our churches about what God is doing in Israel today, and for the first time to most of them, being surprised at the lovely reception they have received. We had to learn not to be afraid to share our opinions and to have the courage to cross the great divide to meet one another at the bridge.

Set Free from the Curse

Then you will know the truth, and the truth will set you free.

John 8:32 (NIV)

The Bible speaks much about blessings and curses. Everyone wants to be blessed and favored by God—not cursed. "Suffice it to say that in nearly four thousand years, no individual and no nation has ever cursed the Jewish people without bringing upon themselves in return the blighting curse of God."[83] One's belief system and actions must align with God's design for the universe.

The true ecclesia will love the God of Israel with all of their hearts and not be ashamed to say that He is Israel's God, which they now follow. Truth must lead each one of us. We need to make certain we are in the right place of worship that understands the Jewish people and is willing to teach the whole Bible. Praying for Israel, supporting Israel practically, and learning about our Hebraic foundations are ways to show our love. We must play our part in helping to set many free from Christian antisemitism, which continues to permeate some sections of the church. Even if we do not consider ourselves to be part of an organized church, we still must choose to love one another as we are commanded.

The Beatitudes and parables we learned in our youth should be retaught in context or content. In other words, who was Jesus praising or rebuking, and why? What were His surroundings at the time? Jesus used many Jewish idioms in expressing what He was trying to get across. Other similar examples, such as "An eye for an eye, a tooth for a tooth" (Matthew 5:38), were often taken literally, rather than examining why He used that Jewish idiom for a particular story. Looking behind the meaning of the words is like moving from an elementary school into a university classroom.

Scripture reveals that gentiles who are in Jesus were once outside the pale. By the shedding of His blood, the Lamb of God has brought both Jew and gentile inside the circle of God's love. We are now part of one nation, and the wall which kept us apart, the hostile dividing wall, Jesus broke down: "For he himself is our peace, who has made the two groups one and has destroyed the barrier, the dividing wall of hostility" (Ephesians 2:14, NIV). However, religious dogmas put the wall back up with its betrayal and breach of trust toward the family of Jesus.

In the Jewish Temple, gentiles were never allowed past the outer court. They used to be utter strangers to God's community of faith and totally excluded from the Commonwealth of Israel. They were also strangers from the covenants of promise founded on the Word of God, without hope and without the God of Israel. There was nothing to look forward to, with regard to heaven, until the Jewish Messiah Jesus came into billions of hearts (Ephesians 2:13). However, by God's grace, gentiles have been admitted an audience with the God of Israel because of the death and resurrection of Jesus that opened the pathway for them into the Holy of Holies (Ephesians 2:12-15). We are a part of redeemed Israel to come, the Israel of God, but we, too, must obey God's commands.

Had we all known and understood Paul's words, how wonderful it would have been if we could have blessed the Jewish people, who were struggling to rebuild their homeland, and be a part of their restoration.

When the Jewish people suffered, Christians should have chosen to suffer alongside them. Too few chose that route of integrity and conscience. We are still trying to find answers to questions in the minds of children and grandchildren of Jewish relatives whom our community of faith betrayed. However, erasing the past is not as easy as we may think. We must make amends for the distorted image of Christ that was given to our Jewish brothers and sisters for twenty centuries. We must repair the damage done to so many in His name.

Love is unconditional kindness. Love was not supposed to parade itself clothed in spiritual pride. Unfortunately, most Christians crushed the heart of Jesus. Pure love is the greatest, and we are to pursue it. "Though I speak with the tongues of men and of angels, but have not love, I have become sounding brass or a clanging cymbal" (1 Corinthians 13:1).

For Christians to receive the Abrahamic blessing, we must raise the cup of kindness. God allowed "thorns and thistles" to grow in many a congregation throughout the ages, and the church forfeited many spiritual blessings.

Years ago, I wrote an elementary phonetic picture booklet for our youngsters entitled "Tell the Children." It explains to our children in pictures the role of the Jewish people. It came about as I had read a small booklet someone placed into my hands, entitled "Hatred Is Sacred." This small booklet clearly illustrated, throwing light upon, how the lives of young Arab children are indoctrinated, from the day they are born, to hate the Jewish people. The title gave away the philosophy behind the movement, which still trains influenceable young minds, and that is that a hostile heart toward the "enemy" (the Jewish people) is somehow spiritual. I was so taken aback that I felt if someone could write such a booklet to teach children to hate the Jewish people, then I needed to write a booklet to show the delusion of this belief and to give the reasons why we, as Christians, cannot accept that dogma. Instead, teach our children that love is more sacred!

The book was a very fundamental sketch of the story of the Jewish people in a phonetic and artistic drawing design, something like a coloring book. I never realized that for years, people all over the world copied this little book, used it as a coloring book, and taught about the Jewish people. I will never know the fruit of that labor, but I would love to talk with some of the children, who are now grown, ask them what they learned from that book and if the message makes a difference in how they see Jewish people today.

It is still a great tool for teaching children in our Sunday school classes. It finishes up with guiding youngsters on how to react if they know Jewish friends or victims of antisemitic abuse are being attacked verbally and how they, as Christians, should respond. (This booklet is still available on the CFI website.)

I was impressed with the following true story written in *Blessing or Cursing: You Can Choose* by Dr. Derek Prince. It proves that once a person gets free from an antisemitic heart, no matter who they are, they can then be prepared to receive the cup of blessing from the Lord. Herewith is the story of someone who arrived at a specific conclusion. This true story is truly one of many who have been set free from the curse of hatred of the Jewish people.

> My name is Nabil Haddad. I am a Palestinian Arab born in Haifa in 1938 to Christian Arab parents. I remember that from my earliest childhood, I would always go to bed depressed. I became determined to find a way to be happy. I knew my parents loved me, but that didn't change my unhappiness. I became convinced that if I could become rich and successful, then I would be happy. That became my goal. In 1948, the fighting between the Arabs and the Jews began. Our whole family moved to Lebanon. In the late 1950s, I went to the United States to college. So, in America, I set out to achieve my goal of becoming rich and successful through education and business...I became an American citizen, started a family and began a franchise of McDonald's restaurants.

By the age of thirty, I was a millionaire. However, the depression had not left me...nothing worked. Finally, I began to ask questions: who is this Man Jesus? Who is this One that people still talk about 2,000 years after His death? I found someone who could show me how to pray, I repented and asked Jesus into my life. A few months later, I was baptized in the Holy Spirit. Now I had the answer—I no longer went to bed depressed. But my life was still not right. My business continued to go downhill. Again I confronted the Lord...and within ten months I was bankrupt. A little later I went to Ft. Lauderdale for a seminar called, "Curses: Cause and Cure" taught by Derek Prince. I learned that many areas of my life were under a curse—financial, physical, not enjoying my children, etc. I remembered the same kinds of problems in my father's life and in the lives of other family members. On the third day, when Derek led the few hundred people in a prayer to be set free from curses, I stood up. For eight straight hours, I was being released from curses. When I asked the Lord what I was being delivered from He showed me witchcraft and many other specific problems. One day as I was worshipping, I said, "How great You are! You created the universe and everything in it!" The Lord asked me if I really believed that. I said, "Yes, Lord." He said, "What about the Jewish people? You still hold resentment in your heart against them." I remembered how my whole family had always cursed the Jews. I was trained to hate them from my earliest years. Now, in the presence of the Lord I said, "I renounce any resentment in my heart toward the Jewish people. I forgive them!" Immediately, something changed inside me. Shortly after this I saw that God in His Word had told Abraham, the father of the Jew, "I'll bless those who bless you and curse those who curse you" (Genesis 12:3). Then I realized that my finances had not been under a blessing, but under a curse—a curse of insufficiency—since 1982. When I was released from the curse of antisemitism and the curse of insufficiency that went with it, my income has always exceeded my expenses and my needs.[84]

In the same manner that Nabil repented and changed his mindset that led to a truly blessed life is the way each individual can find true peace and favor with God. The blessings of Abraham are offered to the Christians through Jesus, our mediator.

Early one bright sunny morning, the door of our second ministry office, on Natan Hanavi in Jerusalem, a young religious Jewish man, walked through our doors. He walked over to the reception desk, which I was standing nearby, and handed me a paper entitled a *Discourse on the Restoration of the Jews*, delivered at the Tabernacle church in New York City, on two occasions in 1844. Whatever the various historical accounts of this man's life, Mordecai Manuel Noach, stood behind the pulpit of the Tabernacle church on 18 October and 8 December 1844.[85] The nineteen-page discourse delivered to me came by way of a great-grandson of Mr. Noach. Christians called him a "prophetic preacher," but the Jewish world used the word "prophet" who through his voice, his words reverberated throughout the auditorium, and into the hearts, of a large New York Christian congregation years before Israel became a state, voted in by the United Nations, on 14 May 1948.

He took the opportunity to make the emotional appeal to an audience he thought should be caring for and blessing his Jewish people. He asked the Christians present to be active in working to help his people to get to the land of their forefathers. Keep in mind: this was long before 1948. This prophetic voice wanted to be heard in relation to the cry to help them take possession of their ancient heritage. I have included portions of the discourse here in this chapter in order for our ears to hear this man foretelling of events before they happened. What he envisioned was way before the dry bones came alive. It should speak to us that we really do have work to do—work that will be considered a *blessing* in God's eyes. If you have never thought about blessing Israel, I hope this booklet will inspire and test you to ascertain the worth of the Jewish people to the world, the significant role they play in the end times, and the great debt we owe to them, for all we possess as Christians was given by them.

We have a plethora of financial assets in the Christian world and prayer power available to us that has barely been tapped. Since we cannot take even a penny with us when we leave this world, we have wonderful opportunities now to meet the many needs of *aliyah*, restoration, resettling, rebuilding of lives and supplementing the lives of disadvantaged, victims of terror attacks, and many more in the land who lack the finances to advance in life.

Christian Friends of Israel offers you that opportunity. Whether you have resources, great or small, God will weigh the balances when He hands out the rewards. I'm sure He will examine each window of opportunity that we were given in our time. Will the worldwide Christian community in the nations work alongside God and cooperate with His plans and purposes He has for chosen people, or will we continue to spend our financial resources on perishable "things" that have little value in the kingdom of God comes down to a choice which only you and I can make.

Mordecai's Noah's voice still can be heard in the sacred place of our hearts, as if he is still standing in the pulpit at the Tabernacle on that Friday, in January, and again on Monday, in December 1844. His prophetic words can still be captured if we listen closely. It is as if he has reappeared, delivering, for the first time, the God-inspired tidings of one born to speak of future events.

I have long desired, my friends and countrymen, for an opportunity to appear before you...I have been anxious to appeal to you, citizens and Christians, on behalf of the chosen and beloved people of Almighty God...to feel for their sufferings and woes; to extend to them your powerful protection and undivided support in accomplishing the fulfillment of their destiny, and aiding to restore them to the land of their forefathers and the possession of their ancient heritage...While the Almighty raised up, enlarged, and extended the Gentile Church, gave to it power and dominion, he threw the mantle of his Divine protection over His chosen people, and has preserved them amid unheard-of dangers to this very day, the same people whom He had brought out of Egyptian bondage.[86]

These are scriptures Mordecai noted before he continued his dissertation:

"He will set up a banner for the nations, And will assemble the outcasts of Israel, And gather together the dispersed of Judah From the four corners of the earth" (Isaiah 11:12). "I will plant them in their land, And no longer shall they be pulled up From the land I have given them," Says the LORD your God" (Amos 9:15). "Strangers shall stand and feed your flocks, And the sons of the foreigner Shall be your plowmen and your vinedressers" (Isaiah 61:5).

On these unfulfilled predictions, my friends, rest the happiness of the human race; and you are heirs to this new covenant, partners in the compact sharers in the glory. Understand these prophecies distinctly: they relate to the literal, and not to the spiritual restoration of the Jews, as many believe. Above all, you that believe in the predictions of your apostles, you who believe in the second coming of the Son of Man to Jerusalem, to Zion, to the beloved city of hope and promise.

Within the last twenty-five years great revolutions have occurred in the East...Palestine, thus placed between the Russian possessions and Egypt, reverts to its legitimate proprietors, and for the safety of the surrounding nations...and with their aid and agency the land of Israel passes once more into the possession of the descendants of Abraham...and Christian and Jew will together, on Mount Zion, raise their voices in praise of Him whose covenant with Abraham was to endure forever, and in whose seed all the nations of the earth are to be blessed...I propose...for all the Christian societies who take an interest in the fate of Israel, to assist in their restoration by aiding to colonize the Jews in Judea; the progress may be slow, but the result will be certain...hitherto they have had no protecting influence, no friendly hand stretched forth to aid them...This, my friends, may be the glorious result of any liberal movement you may be disposed to make in promoting the final destiny of the chosen people...Let us unfurl the standard...If we do not move when He disposes events to correspond with the fulfillment of His promises and the prediction of his prophetic, we leave undone that which He entails upon us as a duty to perform, and the work is not accomplished, the day of deliverance has not arrived. He has spoken—He has promised...It is our duty...to see it executed...But we cannot move alone in the great work of the restoration. The power and influence of our Christian brethren, which now control the destinies of the world, must be invoked in carrying out this most interesting project...I am persuaded...that consummation of a great and providential ensign in the union of the Jews and Gentiles...can alone be looked for after the restoration of the Jews to the land which the Lord gave to them for an everlasting possession. It is your duty, men and Christians, to aid us peaceably...to repossess the land of our fathers, to which we have a legal, equitable, perpetual right, by a covenant...that power and glory which were once our own, you now possess: the banner of the Crescent floats where the standard of Judah was once displayed: it is for you to unfurl it again on Mount Zion...you believe in the second coming of Jesus of Nazareth. That second advent, Christians, depends upon you. It cannot come to pass, by your own admission, until the Jews are restored, and restored in their unconverted state. If He is again to appear, it must be to His own people, and in the land of his birth and his affections—on the spot where he preached, and prophesied and died."[87]

Well spoken. If our generation only heeds this advice, many might be set free from the curse of calling hatred "sacred" and live up to the calling we have to stay close to our Jewish brethren and to bless them in whatever way we are able. May we all cease listening to biased and hateful talk about Israel and its people, stop believing everything negative we hear through antisemitic reports, and be wise enough to spot fake news and dishonest reporting about Israel. Anyone can ask God to help them acquire freedom from the curse of antisemitism, and when they do, great things will begin to happen. Thank God for the millions that have already done so.

Unsung Heroes of Christianity

And everyone who competes for the prize is temperate in all things. Now they do it to obtain a perishable crown, but we for an imperishable crown. Therefore I run thus: not with uncertainty. Thus I fight: not as one who beats the air.

1 Corinthians 9:25-26

An unsung hero is someone who has made an important and meaningful contribution to the welfare of others, someone whose bravery and courage may be unknown or never acknowledged. There are many unsung Christian heroes in the annals of history, including records of the time during World War II that few know about. These were people who were willing to take a chance on getting arrested or even killed for shielding a Jewish life.

As these heroes were not afraid to strike a blow to their future lives, it is going to take courageous Christians who will not be afraid of standing up and backing the Jewish people when it comes to historical antisemitism, institutional dogmas, doctrines, and teachings that up until the latter part of the last century, were above criticism. That can no longer be allowed. Empowering the Bible to challenge any questionable doctrine or creed is completely in order. The Bible must be our final guide and absolute truth from which we draw our beliefs.

Our unsung Christian heroes of the past and present will need to be willing to risk their lives for the Jewish people. It was a Jew in the flesh who gave His life for me. Can I do any less for Him and His people? Israel is not perfect. It has many flaws and certainly has not yet risen to be the spiritual light it is destined to be, but I say this determinedly: Scripture tells us that it will be a "light to the nations" (Isaiah 49:6). That is enough for me because Jesus told us "every jot and tittle of the Torah" will be fulfilled (Matthew 5:18). Therefore, we are charged with a sacred task, like the apostle Shaul (Paul).

We need to inspire our leaders and readers to seek and win an imperishable crown in the next life to come.

> It is not a material crown, like the wreath of fading leaves. It is a crown of righteousness and of life and is, consequently, in its nature, immortal. It is worn in the land of incorruption and immortality. It blooms perennially in the atmosphere of heaven.[88]

There are many testimonies of righteous gentiles (Christians) on the internet to tap into reading about their bravery and courage. Some outstanding ones come to mind, such as Raoul Wallenberg, a Swedish architect, businessman, diplomat, and humanitarian who was widely revered for saving tens of thousands of Hungarian Jews during WWII. Major General Orde Wingate, a British military intelligence officer during the British Mandate, passionately embraced the prophetic vision of Jewish redemption in the land of Israel. William Heckler, a British restorationist, Anglican clergyman and advocate against antisemitism, and Corrie Ten Boom of the Netherlands. She and her family helped Jewish people escape the Nazi Holocaust and are credited with saving nearly 800 Jewish lives. Dietrich Bonhoeffer of Germany was a pastor of the Confessing Church, theologian, and anti-Nazi dissident, who was hanged for aiding the Jews.

These were some of the well-known, courageous believers in Jesus who stepped out of their comfort zone and were willing to take a stand for truth, whatever it personally cost them. Gustav Scheller of Switzerland, a successful businessman, and negotiator, gave up his successful tourism businesses in Europe to bring Jewish people home in the first ships that ever sailed the seas in modern times. There are so many more, but many are known only to God and are in His book of records.

These believing friends of Israel represented their nations as "sheep nations," obeying the Great Shepherd of our souls. They saw the needs of the Jewish people and lived their lives according to God's commands. Righteous judgment will come for all people, including the Jewish homeland, but it is for God to judge His people and not the church. Certainly, the fate of nations hangs in the balance, and it may be proven that Genesis 12:3 was connected to their principles in life regarding the Jews.

It has always taken courage to swim against the tide of antisemitism and the all-too-common prevailing tendency to have anti-Jewish opinions. The truth of the danger Israel confronts on a daily basis must be told by Christians, especially those living in the Jewish nation.

Mordecai's counsel to Queen Esther was

> For if you remain completely silent at this time, relief and deliverance will arise for the Jews from another place, but you and your father's house will perish. Yet who knows whether you have come to the kingdom for such a time as this.
>
> Esther 4:14

For those of us who stand with Israel, persecution may come in the form of laughter, mocking, or derogatory remarks, but we must weather them. Even if alone—stand. We must not let go of the Genesis 12:3 promise. I have written what I have written to help the church see the light of God's love, plans, and purposes for His chosen people.

Israel has been a vicious bone in the throat of antisemitic nations and very much in the throat of Islam. Now we are reading about the persecution of Christians in many fanatic Islamic nations. Alongside those stories come testimonies of untold numbers of Muslims turning to Jesus. Many have had dreams and visions of Him or a personal visit from above. Immediately, when they turn to Jesus, they feel a love for the Jewish people. For some, it is more difficult, but when submitted to Him, their hearts are changed.

The bone of contention with Israel seems to be stuck in the windpipe of a great deal of mankind, and it has proven hard to remove. Only the spirit of the Lord Jesus can truly remove it. As stated, much of the church believed that Israel failed to carry out her mission from God. Therefore, they believed God was finished with it. Without understanding God's plans and purposes for the nation, mankind continues to choke on its lack of understanding.

Something new is being born. This mindset goes back to the moment in which Jacob received the name "Israel."

> Jacob was left alone; and a Man wrestled with him until the breaking of day. Now when He saw that He did not prevail against him, He touched the socket of his hip; and the socket of Jacob's hip was out of joint as He wrestled with him. And He said, "Let Me go, for the day breaks." But he said "I will not let You go unless You bless me!" So He said to him, "What is your name?" He said, "Jacob." And He said, "Your name shall no longer be called Jacob, but Israel; for you have struggled with God and with men and have prevailed."
>
> Genesis 32:24-28

We may find ourselves limping, as did Jacob, but his persistence and courage became the basis of his new name and identity. May the coming church in the end times have a new name and identity coming alongside Israel and being true brothers walking across a bridge with hands outstretched. The long parting of the ways must end, and may we see it with our eyes.

Israel became a mighty warrior that grew stronger with each conflict and catastrophe. They seem to have found ways of turning every curse into a blessing, for God has chosen Israel to give testimony to mankind that "out of suffering can come great blessings, if you wrestle with it long enough and with unshakeable faith."[89]

For every Jewish life that suffered during periods of Christian antisemitic rampage, there was a remnant of valiant and heroic citizens of the nations who would not participate in such wickedness. Their bones also lie in church cemeteries. Not all rescuers were Christians by new birth, but there was a remnant of ordinary men and women who acted with personal integrity toward their Jewish friends and neighbors, who believed in Jesus and did what was right. We salute them.

Among the count known only to God were 5,000 Christians in Le Chambon, France, who protected the Jewish people at the peril of their own lives. They fed them, took them into their homes, and protected them from the Nazis. No one in their village ever turned away a single Jewish refugee or betrayed one "Old Testament," a code name, that some of them were called.[90]

Andre Trocme, the Protestant pastor of the village church, had taught his congregants well. The Jewish people fleeing the Nazis came to Pastor Trocme's door first. His acts of kindness became a beacon of hope for thousands. Members of his congregation followed suit. In a conversation with one of the villagers, he said, "As soon as the soldiers [Nazis] left, we would go into the forest and sing a song. When our Jewish guests heard the song, they knew it was safe to come home." They are among the heroes honored by the State of Israel, on the Avenue of the Righteous, at the Yad Vashem Memorial site in Jerusalem.[91]

The recorded number of honorable Christians is far fewer than what we would like to see and too few to heartily applaud with gusto, but those who did come to the aid of the Jewish people are to be praised for their actions. God does know those of conscience who chose to be moral and decent. They acted as safe havens for the hated and hunted from Jewish communities. Job said, "These ten times you have reproached me; You are not ashamed that you have wronged me" (Job 19:3).

While many in the church ignored or participated, there were some who helped hide the persecuted Jews. Fear was a way of life for those who chose to protect. Even though in our cemeteries lay untold stories of numbers of people who missed opportunities to bring blessings to the Jewish people, especially during times of genocidal attempts to annihilate the entire race, there are names on tombstones of those who stood for righteousness. They sought the welfare of God's chosen people and knew they were touching something precious to God's heart.

We can now begin in our own communities, or wherever we are, to be a remnant that fears God and acts nobly when confronted with the truth. Let us find our consciences in a time of great danger and human depravity, especially for the Jews and our fellow Christians—both of which are being persecuted for their faith in the one true God.

If more Christians stand in the gap for Jewish neighbors, "Oh, that one might plead for a man with God, As a man pleads for his neighbor" (Job 16:21), we can change the course of history. We must not become strangers to the Jewish communities ever again. The scriptures prophesy the worst of times before the Messiah's second coming, a time when many nations will fight against Israel (Jeremiah 30:7). At the right time, Messiah's feet will descend on the Mount of Olives with the ultimate stand for His people to defeat the opposing nations (Zechariah 14).

For any wrong feelings, please take them to the Lord and ask Him what to do about them. "And if indeed I have erred, My error remains with me. If indeed you exalt yourselves against me, And plead my disgrace against me" (Job 19:4-5). The root of the matter of antisemitism may still be there. God hates it. Let us deal with it now.

And so we may visit our cemeteries where lay untold stories of believers who missed their opportunities to bring blessings to the Jewish people, especially during difficult times. For those who sought the welfare of God's chosen people, we will always remain grateful that they took the high road and not the low road. They knew they were touching something precious to

God. They did not take the command of God in Genesis 12:3 lightly but took it to heart. Their names as Christians are not only written in heaven because of their faith in Jesus but because they loved not their own lives to death (Revelation 12:11) and grabbed ahold of the principle and the promise!

Roll Call of the Nations

When the Son of Man comes in His glory, and all the holy angels with Him, then He will sit on the throne of His glory. All the nations will be gathered before Him, and He will separate them one from another, as a shepherd divides his sheep from the goats.

Matthew 25:31-32

One day in the near future, in Jerusalem, this event will happen. We will call it the Roll Call of the nations. Roll Call, generally, is the process of checking attendance through the calling out and ticking off of names. On that day, the Lord will separate the sheep nations (those who performed righteous acts) from the goat nations (those who rebelled and committed wicked deeds against the Jewish people). The separation will be final and without appeal. It will be a time when the final ruling is the Lord's. Neither moral relativism, secularism, nor humanism will prevail on that day. "Let all those who hate Zion Be put to shame and turned back [...] Neither let those who pass by them say 'The blessing of the LORD be upon you; We bless you in the name of the LORD!'" (Psalm 129:5, 8).

I have no doubt that we are in the final days when the Spirit actually returns to Jerusalem. When the King of Kings returns to Jerusalem to set up His Father's kingdom for a thousand-year reign, we will learn of a great judgment day. Yes, the city of Jerusalem will one day be host to the most prestigious and, yet, chilling Roll Call in the history of the world. An ominous day of reckoning looms on the horizon.

The most powerful, as well as the weakest, of nations will be summoned before the King of Kings when He sits on His Throne to govern. Genesis 12:3 has a significant bearing on the ultimate future judgment of nations.[92] We can see in prophecy how nations who turn against Israel will pay a heavy price, total destruction. Nations that treated the Jewish people with love and mercy and those who looked down on them, regarding them with disdain, will be adjudicated during the King's separating of the sheep and goat nations. The Words of Jesus regarding the choice to bless or curse is echoed herein, symbolized by calling them sheep and goat nations.

The reality of the Jewish predicament in Martin Luther's time was enough to support his theology that God was finished with the Jews—but not now, not today with the resurrection of the Jewish people, the return to their homeland, and the development of one of the most beautiful nations in the world. "Nor will I let you hear the taunts of the nations anymore, nor bear the reproach of the peoples anymore, nor shall you cause your nation to stumble anymore, says the Lord GOD" (Ezekiel 36:15).

Scripture reveals that the whole world will face this forthcoming watershed moment, based upon their siding for or against God and His chosen people. As previously stated, God will punitively judge and purge nations into two separate categories, sheep and goats (Ezekiel 34:17). One can only imagine the tension that will prevail as all await their verdict.

By equating today's nations with nations of the agrarian world of the Bible, the Great Shepherd, who was acquainted with the landscape and farming communities of His time, painted a mental picture for us to better understand this coming day of separation of people groups. Examining the attributes of sheep and goats might help us to gain a better understanding of His biblical metaphors. Sheep usually follow a shepherd. However, goats often go their own way. Because of the independent nature of goats, they easily find themselves in contention with the shepherd. Fences that hold sheep will not necessarily hold goats.

We must grasp the reality of the roll call. Nations will not be able to bargain earthly possessions nor flaunt national superiority. That will not make a difference. The sheep nations reflect Jesus' character and have displayed it throughout history. The goat nations have not. The division came as a result of deeds of kindness and mercy. The King welcomes the righteous to their inheritance on the basis of their altruistic, compassionate deeds toward the Jews. He identifies such benevolence as if it were done to Him (Matthew 25:40).

Tradition can become so ingrained that we will not allow the Bible to challenge us. Will we cooperate with God's will in reuniting Jesus with His brothers to fulfill His plans and purposes? Somehow God is going to purify His Body across the world and open up eyes to see Jesus not as the founder of the Christian church and as the first Christian or the first Catholic.

We can picture the King of kings sitting upon His throne with the nations before Him. His decree determines who may or may not be an heir of His kingdom. The basis of the King's judgment is how the nations treated "His brethren" (Matthew 25:37-40). Loving our fellow man and doing good in our service to others is a fruit of knowing the Master in Christianity.

Jesus gave Jerusalem its great importance. He was brought to this city as a child and presented in the temple. He took part in their feasts and was captured, tried, crucified, and buried here. The most glorious of all events was that this city saw His resurrection and ascension. In the light of predestined events, this city will receive Him as King. Every true believer must look to developments in the world related to God's plan to establish His kingdom within these walls.

The name "Jerusalem" appears 669 times in the Hebrew Bible; in the New Testament, "Jerusalem" is mentioned 154 times. No other city has the same fate. One day this city will host His Majesty on its highest peak. The Temple Mount will one day be the resting place for His feet as He rules the nations on the dust of their ground. Secular architects and urban planners may not be aware of the spiritual importance of their current work, but plans are being made to beautify the holy city.

Satan hates God's plan of redemption and will do all he can to prevent Jerusalem from being God's eternal throne. He has desired the worship of the world for himself. It was not until 1010 BC before King David arose to defeat the Jebusites. By the providence of God, he made the city his administrative capital. When he brought the ark into the city, he intended to build a temple for God where the ark could be kept permanently, but David was not allowed to build the temple because he was a warrior. David's son, Solomon, built the temple that was to become the focus of Jewish attention from then until now.

After 2,000 years of exile, the nation of Israel was reborn in a day, May 14, 1948.[93] Jerusalem, then known as "Palestine," captivated the world's attention. Israel entered the world's center stage. Battles ensued with intensity.

In May 1948, Transjordan occupied East Jerusalem, dividing the city and driving thousands of Jews into exile. The city was divided for nineteen years. Israel built its capital in West Jerusalem, and Transjordan occupied the eastern section. In 1950, Jordan annexed all of the area west of Jordan, including East Jerusalem. From 1948 to 1967, the city was divided between Israel and Jordan. The city became two armed camps, saturated with concrete walls and bunkers, barbed-wire fences, minefields, and other military fortresses. Jordan denied Israel access to the temple wall. June 6, 1967, God kept the appointment with His people and returned the holy city to Jewish jurisdiction in response to faithful prayers for the past 2,000 years.

The Almighty clearly placed His signature on Jerusalem in preparation for His coming kingship. Neither Mecca nor

Rome, but only Jerusalem will be "glory on earth" because of the Messiah (Isaiah 62: 7).

It may amaze many of us who are learning for the first time the permanence of Israel, even in the world to come. Replacement theology and supersessionism would find it hard to believe that Revelation 21:12 informs us that in the heavenly city of the new heaven and earth which was descending out of heaven (Revelation 21:1) literally has a "wall great and high, and had twelve gates, and at the gates twelve angels, and names written thereon, which are the names of the twelve tribes of the children of Israel." As we read on to verse fourteen, we see twelve gates with the names of the apostles of the Lamb written above (who were also Jews).

The door frames with the Jewish names are important to note because they represent a threshold, an entrance, or a gateway that one has to pass under to enter while crossing over the threshold. If there be any trace of prejudice toward God's chosen people, the Jewish people of Genesis 12:3 is not to be taken lightly. It would be troublesome to visualize even one antisemitic heart being allowed into God's kingdom. Why do I say that? Because the Bible says this about the coming kingdom: "outside are the dogs and anyone who believes a lie" (Revelation 22:15).

There is an urgent need for a waking up in the church. It is imperative that it learn to understand that Jerusalem was and will be the place of holy worship for the Jewish people one day, but also for all nations. Churchgoers have to get on the Jewish train heading for Jerusalem. Jesus' first disciples foresaw the restoration of Jerusalem, "Lord, will You at this time restore the kingdom to Israel?" (Acts 1:6). Yeshua told them not to worry about it but continue with the work He had given them to do—carry the message of the Messiah out into the world.

Israel is sacred territory to God and the Jewish people. Some speak of it as God's timepiece, with Jerusalem being the minute hand and the Temple Mount His second hand. Jerusalem is the holiest city in Judaism and Christianity. Jewish religious regulations state that prayers should be said face-to-face toward this city and especially the Temple Mount.

It is noteworthy that the Messiah will not return to any great capitals in the world. He will not come to Washington, not to London, Paris, Moscow, or Beijing. He won't even come to Rome with its Christian communities, nor to Geneva. He will come to Jerusalem. This must be a problem for all those who do not see the hand of God in the restoration of the state of Israel and the capital Jerusalem. Jerusalem will look very Jewish during the Millennium with a Jewish temple and sacrifices. (Ezekiel, chapters forty-two through forty-seven, tells us all about it.) Jesus will rule from the throne of David. The Feast of Tabernacles will require attendance to receive the Lord's favor of rain during the Millennium (Zechariah 14:17-19).

From Jerusalem, the Jews were scattered all over the world in AD 70, and they have now returned to Jerusalem. It is the inhabitants of Jerusalem who, when the Spirit of grace and prayer is poured out on them, will bring the entire nation to look to Him "whom they have pierced" (Zechariah 12:10). Those blessed and pierced feet will one day tread the dust of the Mount of Olives in Jerusalem.

> From her lips He will hear these wonderful words of greeting: Blessed be he who comes in the name of the Lord. With the return of the Messiah the circle will come full. All human history, and especially Jewish history, will have found its fulfillment.[94]

Because it is God's decision that Jerusalem will be the place of the Eternal King's coronation, it must be ours too. Every true Christian has a serious responsibility to Jerusalem. This most sacred of all properties is only a few kilometers away from our house. Sometimes I imagine the Messiah's sanctuary on the mountain east of our home. All the splendor of the past and the future swells in the emotions of my heart. The essence of Jerusalem, which has remained steadfast despite space and time, makes it the most fantastic of all cities in the world to live in.

Long embedded in the spiritual consciousness of Jews and Christians, she will always be the mother of all cities. Rebuilding the temple has been the desire of the Jewish people for decades. The words "Next year in Jerusalem" (*l'shanah haba'ah b'yerushalim*) have crossed the lips of almost every Jewish person at some point. Thousands of worshipers stand on Jerusalem's western wall, where Jewish festivals take place throughout the year.

The land of Israel really is of special value, but Jerusalem is the crown jewel. It is a royal diadem in the hand of the Lord. This is the reason why Jews and Christians worldwide feel a pull in their hearts and cannot avoid taking the journey, to then experience a spiritual surge of emotion as soon as their feet are inside the gates of Jerusalem. Many have the feeling of "coming home" when they touch the historic walls. Jerusalem has a spiritual hope in her heart that enlivens the human spirit. "I will make them and the places all around My hill a blessing; and I will cause showers to come down in their season; there shall be showers of blessing" (Ezekiel 34:26).

It will remain a symbol of hope for all who place their faith in the God of Israel. The splendor of the divine presence will be in this city again...and the light of His revived *menorah* will illuminate the earth with eternal peace forever. "The city had no need of the sun or of the moon to shine in it, for the glory of God illuminated it. The Lamb is its light" (Revelation 21:23).

Since we are in the time period of the "restoration of all things" (Acts 3:21), God forbid that anyone in the church be too proud to admit they might be seriously wrong in how they treated Israel and to ask forgiveness of God. He loves each of us and stands willingly, ready to pardon. With Israel back in the land, the Roll Call of the Nations is soon to come. Let us make sure we are standing on the side of the blessed. "And this is the promise that He has promised us—eternal life" (1 John 2:25).

Therefore, we as Christians must understand that He is not returning to Jerusalem to transform the Jewish nation into a "gentile Christian church." The Holy Spirit will work with Israel to graft them back into their own cultivated olive tree (Romans 11:24). The missing link in our faith (Israel) and those redeemed from the nations will become "one new humanity" in which the kingdom of God will bring us together under the Lordship of Messiah Yeshua (Jesus). All will hear the law going forth from Zion (Isaiah 2:3), and it will be interpreted for all of mankind not by man but by the voice of the Messiah speaking forth the Father's words to all of mankind. Those who stand with Israel and follow God's principles now will become one family in God's eternal kingdom. "For assuredly, I say to you, till heaven and earth pass away, one jot or one tittle will by no means pass from the law till all is fulfilled" (Matthew 5:18).

It is my profound yearning to see the worldwide church grasp the full understanding of the eternal principle and the ensuing promise of God. For all who would help reconnect the missing link in our faith to their personal walk with the one true God, it will assuredly place the church back on the path of blessing and to God's heart.

Notes

1 Doug Feavel, *A Storyteller's Anthology: 26 Inspiring Character Portraits For Our Time* (Abbotsford: Aneko Press, 2015), 269.

2 "Christians" article in *Wikipedia*, March 7, 2021, https://en.wikipedia.org/w/index.php?title=Christians&oldid=1010759254.

3 Stephen Douglas Wilson, "Where Was Jesus Tried? | Baptist Press," https://www.baptistpress.com/, April 1, 2015, https://www.baptistpress.com/resource-library/news/where-was-jesus-tried/.

4 Ben Sales, "Archaeologist Believes He's Found Site of Jesus's Trial by Pontius Pilate," accessed October 11, 2021, http://www.timesofisrael.com/archaeologist-believes-hes-found-site-of-jesuss-trial-by-pontius-pilate/.

5 "New King James Version (NKJV) - Version Information - BibleGateway.Com," v. (see Isaiah 60:12, Joel 3:1-2, Zechariah 2:8; Matthew 25:40), accessed March 8, 2021, https://www.biblegateway.com/versions/New-King-James-Version-NKJV-Bible/.

6 "New King James Version (NKJV) - Version Information - BibleGateway.Com," v. (Deuteronomy 32:10; Zechariah 2:8).

7 Gallup Inc., "More U.S. Protestants Have No Specific Denominational Identity," Gallup.com, July 18, 2017, https://news.gallup.com/poll/214208/protestants-no-specific-denominational-identity.aspx.

8 John Parsons, "The Importance of Blessing the Jewish People," accessed October 7, 2021, https://www.hebrew-4christians.com/Articles/Blessing_the_Jews/blessing_the_jews.html.

9 Parsons, "The Importance of Blessing the Jewish People."

10 Derek Prince, *Blessing or Curse: You Can Choose* (Grand Rapids: Chosen Books, 1990), 98.

11 Eli Lizorkin Eyzenbert, "Dr. Eli Lizorkin Eyzenberg - IIBS," Israel Institute of Biblical Studies, accessed March 8, 2021, https://israelbiblicalstudies.com/teacher/eli-lizorkin-eyzenberg/.

12 Jeremy Wiles, "Sing a Little Louder" (Holland: KingdomWorks Studios), accessed March 8, 2021, https://kingdomworks.com/films/sing-a-little-louder/?ims=cw-102416.

13 Prince, *Blessing or Curse: You Can Choose*, 98.

14 "Historical Perspectives," Religion Library - Roman Catholicism, accessed March 8, 2021, https://www.patheos.com/library/roman-catholicism/origins/historical-perspectives.

15 Yonat Shimrom, "Pope Francis Challenged by Israel's Chief Rabbis over His Comments on the Torah," America Magazine, August 27, 2021, https://www.americamagazine.org/politics-society/2021/08/27/pope-francis-judaism-rabbinate-241299.

16 Michael Freund, "Fundamentally Freund: Stop Calling It the 'Old Testament' - The Jerusalem Post," The Jerusalem Post, March 8, 2017, https://www.jpost.com/Opinion/Fundamentally-Freund-Stop-calling-it-the-Old-Testament-483640.

17 Steven Gertz, "Opponents of Allegory," Christian History | Learn the History of Christianity & the Church, accessed March 8, 2021, https://www.christianitytoday.com/history/issues/issue-80/opponents-of-allegory.html.

18 Donald K. McKim, ed., *Historical Handbook of Major Biblical Interpreters*, first edition (Downers Grove: Intervarsity Press, 1998), 58–59.

19 McKim, 58.

20 John Parsons, "Should Christians Celebrate Purim," Hebrews for Christians, February 2010, https://hebrew4christians.com/About_HFC/Site_News/Archive-2010/February/february.html.

21 "Church Councils," Jewish Virtual Library, accessed March 9, 2021, https://www.jewishvirtuallibrary.org/church-councils.

22 Richard Griffin, *They Sang Louder* (Grace Point Publishing, 2013).

23 Prince, *Blessing or Curse: You Can Choose.*

24 Martin Luther, *The Jews and Their Lies* (York, SC: Liberty Bell Publications, 2004).

25 Eli Lizorkin-Eyzenberg, *The Jewish Apostle Paul: Rethinking One of the Greatest Jews That Ever Lived.*, ed. Ludmila Lizorkina, n.d., 82.

26 Claire Pfann, *Who Is My Brother*, accessed September 21, 2021, https://jcstudies.store/who-is-my-brother-vital-lessons-from-the-acts-of-the-apostles/.

27 "New King James Version (NKJV) - Version Informa-

tion - BibleGateway.Com," n. Read Deuteronomy, chapter thirty.

28 Efraim Inbar, "The Burden of the 1967 Victory," Begin-Sadat Center for Strategic Studies, April 5, 2017, https://besacenter.org/perspectives-papers/burden-1967-victory/.

29 Steven Lapham, "Ten U.S. Churches Now Sanction Israel—To Some Degree, and with Caveats," WRMEA, March 2019, https://www.wrmea.org/2019-march-april/ten-us-churches-now-sanction-israel-to-some-degree-and-with-caveats.html.

30 "The Social Geography of the BDS Movement and Antisemitism," Begin-Sadat Center for Strategic Studies, August 8, 2019, https://besacenter.org/perspectives-papers/social-geography-bds-antisemitism/.

31 Herbert Lockyer, *All the Men of the Bible* (Grand Rapids: Zondervan, 2016), https://public.ebookcentral.proquest.com/choice/publicfullrecord.aspx?p=5397798.

32 Rabbi David Rosenfeld, "Jethro's Many Names: Ask the Rabbi Response," Ask The Rabbi, accessed March 9, 2021, https://www.aish.com/atr/Jethro-Many-Names.html.

33 Herbert Lockyer, *All the Women of the Bible*, Revised edition (Grand Rapids: Zondervan Academic, 1988), chapter "Rahab."

34 Tamar Meir, "Orpah: Midrash and Aggadah," Jewish Women's Archive, accessed March 9, 2021, https://jwa.org/encyclopedia/article/orpah-midrash-and-aggadah.

35 "New King James Version (NKJV) - Version Information - BibleGateway.Com," v. (2 Samuel 17:27-29; 19:31-40; I

Kings 2:7).

36 Author Leen Ritmeyer, "Bethlehem – the Manger and the Inn," *Ritmeyer Archaeological Design* (blog), December 14, 2014, n. Also see the Eastman Concordance. Scripture reference: Jeremiah 41:17 "And they departed and dwelt in the habitation of Chimham, which is near Bethlehem, as they went on their way to Egypt," https://www.ritmeyer.com/2014/12/14/bethlehem-the-inn-and-the-manger/.

37 "Topical Bible: Zarephath," accessed October 7, 2021, https://biblehub.com/topical/z/zarephath.htm.

38 Yehoshua Schechter, "Trump - a Modern-Day Cyrus? | Americans United with Israel," December 12, 2017, https://americaunitedwithisrael.org/trump-a-modern-day-cyrus/?ios_app=true.

39 Schechter.

40 "Statement by Former President Trump on Jerusalem," U.S. Embassy in Israel, December 7, 2020, http://il.usembassy.gov/statement-by-president-trump-on-jerusalem/.

41 Lockyer, *All the Women of the Bible.*

42 Derek Prince, *Our Debt to Israel* (Baldock, UK: DPM-UK, 2015), 4.

43 Prince, *Our Debt to Israel.*

44 Martin Luther, *The Jews and Their Lies* (York, SC: Liberty Bell Publications, 2004).

45 "The Inquisition," Jewish Virtual Library, accessed March 10, 2021, https://www.jewishvirtuallibrary.org/the-inquisition.

46 "Medieval Inquisition" article in *Wikipedia*, February 4, 2021, https://en.wikipedia.org/w/index.php?title=Medieval_Inquisition&oldid=1004831910.

47 Thomas Madden, "Truth about the Spanish Inquisition," Catholic Culture, accessed March 10, 2021, https://www.catholicculture.org/culture/library/view.cfm?id=5236&repos=1&subrepos=0&searchid=2097068.

48 "The Inquisition."

49 Luther, *The Jews and Their Lies*, 51.

50 Luther, 51.

51 Emily McFarland Miller and Tom Heneghan, "The Nazis Exploited Martin Luther's Legacy," Sojourners, n.d., https://sojo.net/articles/nazis-exploited-martin-luther-s-legacy-berlin-exhibit-highlights-how.

52 Miller and Heneghan.

53 Sharon Sanders, "A Place for My People," *For Zion's Sake*, 2016, https://8fa4931a-5b04-4f8d-a4e9-072a154a4742.filesusr.com/ugd/d3a9e0_edd255c277514f88ab82535341b-b9c79.pdf.

54 "The Opposite of Love Is Not Hate, But Indifference – Quote Investigator," May 21, 2019, https://quoteinvestigator.com/2019/05/21/indifference/.

55 Jonathan Feldstein, "The Holocaust: Remember to Never Forget," Charisma News, accessed September 19, 2021, https://www.charismanews.com/opinion/standing-with-israel/47234-the-holocaust-remember-to-never-forget.

56 Feldstein, "The Holocaust."

57 Patrick Desbois and Paul A Shapiro, *The Holocaust by bullets: a priest's journey to uncover the truth behind the murder of 1.5 million Jews* (Basingstoke: Palgrave Macmillan, 2010).

58 Dr. Yvette Alt Miller, "The Priest Uncovering Hidden Atrocities of the Holocaust," aish.com, November 7, 2015, https://www.aish.com/jw/s/The-Priest-Uncovering-Hidden-Atrocities-of-the-Holocaust.html.

59 Desbois and Shapiro, *The Holocaust by bullets.*

60 Dr. Yvette Miller Miller, "Aish Ha Torah," *The Priest Uncovering Hidden Atrocities of the Holocaust* (blog), November 7, 2015, https://www.aish.com/jw/s/The-Priest-Uncovering-Hidden-Atrocities-of-the-Holocaust.html?s=rab.

61 Dr Yvette Alt Miller, "The Priest Uncovering Hidden Atrocities of the Holocaust," aishcom, November 7, 2015, https://www.aish.com/jw/s/The-Priest-Uncovering-Hidden-Atrocities-of-the-Holocaust.html.

62 Miller, "Hidden Atrocities."

63 Miller.

64 Miller, "Hidden Atrocities."

65 Stephen H Norwood, "Marauding Youth and the Christian Front: Antisemitic Violence in Boston and New York During World War II.," *American Jewish History* 91, no. 2 (2003): 233–67, https://www.jstor.org/stable/23887201?seq=1.

66 Irvin Molotsky, "Red Cross Admits Knowing of the Holocaust During the War," *The New York Times*, December 15, 1996, sec. U.S., https://www.nytimes.com/1996/12/19/

us/red-cross-admits-knowing-of-the-holocaust-during-the-war.html.

67 Luther, *The Jews and Their Lies*, 50–51.

68 John Barrows, "Martin Luther Paved the Way for the Holocaust," The Times of Israel, October 24, 2017, http://blogs.timesofisrael.com/martin-luther-paved-the-way-for-the-holocaust/.

69 Robert W. Ross, *So It Was True: The American Protestant Press and the Nazi Persecution of the Jews*, First Edition (Minneapolis: University of Minnesota Press, 1980).

70 Donna R Edmunds, "There Are 192,000 Holocaust Survivors Living in Israel - The Jerusalem Post," The Jerusalem Post, accessed March 10, 2021, https://www.jpost.com/israel-news/there-are-192000-holocaust-survivors-living-in-israel-614407.

71 Michael L. Brown, *Our Hands Are Stained With Blood: The Tragic Story of the "Church" and the Jewish People* (Shippensburg: Destiny Image Publishers, 1992).

72 "Refusniks," Jewish Virtual Library, accessed March 7, 2021, https://www.jewishvirtuallibrary.org/refusniks.

73 Rachel Sharansky Danziger, "30 Years after Glienicke Bridge," Times of Israel, February 11, 2016, http://blogs.timesofisrael.com/30-years-after-glienicke-bridge/.

74 John K. Roth et al., eds., *Remembering for the Future: The Holocaust in an Age of Genocide* (London: Palgrave Macmillan UK, 2001), https://doi.org/10.1007/978-1-349-66019-3.

75 "Amish Delegation Expresses Remorse to Israel - The Jerusalem Post," The Jerusalem Post, February 11, 2013, https://www.jpost.com/travel/around-israel/amish-delegation-expresses-remorse-to-israel.

76 Courtesy Wikimedia Common, "German Protestant Church Denounces Anti-Semitism of Founder Martin Luther," The Forward, accessed March 10, 2021, https://forward.com/news/breaking-news/324684/german-protestant-church-denounces-anti-semitism-of-founder-martin-luther/.

77 "Anti-Semitic Sculpture to Remain on German Church," BBC News, February 4, 2020, sec. Europe, https://www.bbc.com/news/world-europe-51380171.

78 Alessandra Stanley, "Pope Asks Forgiveness for Errors Of the Church Over 2,000 Years," The New York Times, March 13, 2000, sec. World, https://www.nytimes.com/2000/03/13/world/pope-asks-forgiveness-for-errors-of-the-church-over-2000-years.html.

79 CJCUC, "Orthodox Rabbinic Statement on Christianity," The Center for Jewish–Christian Understanding and Cooperation (blog), December 3, 2015, https://www.cjcuc.org/2015/12/03/orthodox-rabbinic-statement-on-christianity/.

80 Geoff Barnard, Face to Face (self-published, 2017), 139, www.lulu.com.

81 "Gen. Shimon Erem Z"L," Israel Christian Nexus, 2009, http://icnexus.org/gen-shimon-erem.

82 Arthur W. Pink, "Jesus Laid Down His Life?" Chris-

tianity.com, September 20, 2010, https://www.christianity. com/jesus/death-and-resurrection/the-crucifixion/jesus-laid-down-his-life.html.

83 Prince, *Blessing or Curse: You Can Choose*, 94.

84 Prince, *Blessing or Curse: You Can Choose*, 95–96.

85 M. M. Noah, *Discourse on the Restoration of the Jews: Delivered at the Tabernacle*, Oct. 28 and Dec. 2, 1844, Nineteenth Century Collections Online: Religion, Society, Spirituality, and Reform. (New-York: Harper & Brothers, 1845).

86 Noah, *Discourse*.

87 Noah, *Discourse*.

88 J.R. Thomson, "An Incorruptible Crown," Electroic Database, The Pulpit Commentary, accessed March 12, 2021, https://biblehub.com/sermons/auth/thomson/an_incorruptible_crown.htm.

89 "Turning Curses into Blessings," *Sinagoga Edmod J. Safra* (blog), December 28, 2015, http://www.sinagogadeipanema.com.br/en/sermon/shemot/.

90 United States Holocaust Memorial Museum, Washington, DC, "Le Chambon-Sur-Lignon," Holocaust Encyclopedia, accessed March 12, 2021, https://encyclopedia.ushmm.org/content/en/article/le-chambon-sur-lignon.

91 "Protestant Pastor Andre Trocme | Under the Wings of the Church | Themes | A Tribute to the Righteous Among the Nations," Yad Vashem, accessed March 2, 2021, https://www.yadvashem.org/yv/en/exhibitions/righteous/trocme.asp.

92 "New King James Version (NKJV) - Version Informa-

tion - BibleGateway.Com," v. (Zechariah 14:3; Ezekiel 39:12-14).

93 "The State of Israel Is Born," Israel Miistry of Foreign Affairs, accessed March 14, 2021, https://mfa.gov.il/mfa/aboutisrael/israelat50/pages/the%20state%20of%20israel%20is%20born.aspx.

94 Lance Lambert, *Battle for Israel* (Eastbourne, East Sussex: Kingsway Publications, 1988), 113.

Appendix

Who is Christian Friends of Israel

Christians Friends of Israel was organized in 1985 with a special love for God's people and His land. Located in the heart of Jerusalem, we believe that the restoration of the Jewish people to the land of Israel is in accordance with the promises contained in the Word of God and that God's time to favor Zion has begun. We believe that Jesus is both the Messiah of Israel and the Savior of the world, but our stand alongside Israel is not conditional upon her acceptance of our belief. Hosting numerous outreaches, including an in-house distribution center, CFI has touched the lives of hundreds of thousands within the land. The barrier that exists between Jews and Christians is largely due to Christian antisemitism. Therefore, with the help of volunteers and qualified staff, through the years, we have participated in not only the restoration of the Jewish people to the land of Israel but also helping them adjust. Our sincere love for the one true God has enabled us to meet many needs of Holocaust survivors, new immigrants, young soldiers, the medically needy, and those who need a helping hand to sustain the many challenges that Israel faces on a daily basis. It is with supporters from all over the world who share our faith and love that this is made possible.

Christian Friends of Israel Outreaches

Under His Wings: comforting victims of terror (home visits)

David's Shield: supporting brave soldiers in Israel (meeting on bases)

Forsake Them Not: bringing comfort to Holocaust survivors (home visits)

Wall of Prayer: Prayer Department (praying internationally)

Communities under Attack: responding with relief funds to targeted areas of Israel

First Fruits: encouraging the household of faith (congregation visits)

Streams of Blessing: ministry to the destitute and disadvantaged (home visits)

Hope for the Future: helping Jewish Ethiopians (learning center)

Open Gates: assisting new immigrants (Operation Start Up Aliyah Store)

Bridal Salon: helping Jewish brides plan weddings (attending weddings)

Christian Friends Publications:

Watchman Prayer Letter: monthly prayer bulletin, which is available free of charge for praying for Israel in strategic areas.

Raising the Bar Bulletin: monthly bulletin with topical information on an easy-to-learn Hebrew word lesson incorporating it along with prayer for Israel.

Israel Insights: monthly news from Israel written by our media person on the ground, reporting important points for prayer and information.

For Zion's Sake: quarterly ministry showcase reporting stories, testimonies, and how our relationship-building ministry can be supported as partners-in-ministry. This free magazine is available from our website.

CFI Prayer Watch: join with many around the world who are linking into our online Prayer Webinar Watch monthly, meet other believers from around the world who love to pray for Israel, and stay informed in your daily life for intercession and caring for Israel.

For a list of our CFI representatives around the world, see our website.

Christian Friends of Israel

P. O. Box 1813, Jerusalem, 9101701

Telephone: 972-2-623-3778

Fax: 972-2-632-3913

Email: cfi@cfijerusalem.org

www.cfijerusalem.org

Bibliography

The Jerusalem Post, JPost.com. "Amish Delegation Expresses Remorse to Israel - The Jerusalem Post," February 11, 2013. https://www.jpost.com/travel/around-israel/amish-delegation-expresses-remorse-to-israel.

"Anti-Semitic Sculpture to Remain on German Church." BBC News, February 4, 2020, sec. Europe. https://www.bbc.com/news/world-europe-51380171.

Ariel, Gidon, and Bob O'Dell. *Israel First*. Israel: Root Source Press, 2015.

Barnard, Geoff. *Face to Face*. Self-published (www.lulu.com), 2017.

Barrows, John. "Martin Luther Paved the Way for the Holocaust." The Times of Israel, October 24, 2017. http://blogs.timesofisrael.com/martin-luther-paved-the-way-for-the-holocaust/.

Bender, Dave. "Arab-Israeli Priest to UN: 'Israel Only Safe Haven For Christians in Middle East' (video)." Algemeiner.com, September 23, 2014. https://www.algemeiner.com/2014/09/23/arab-israeli-priest-to-un-israel-only-safe-haven-for-christians-in-middle-east-video/.

Brown, Michael L. *Our Hands Are Stained With Blood: The Tragic Story of the "Church" and the Jewish People*. Shippensburg: Destiny Image Publishers, 1992.

"Christians" In *Wikipedia*, March 7, 2021.

https://en.wikipedia.org/w/index.
php?title=Christians&oldid=1010759254.

Jewish Virtual Library. "Church Councils." Accessed March 9, 2021. https://www.jewishvirtuallibrary.org/church-councils.

CJCUC. "Orthodox Rabbinic Statement on Christianity." The Center for Jewish–Christian *Understanding and Cooperation* (blog), December 3, 2015. https://www.cjcuc.org/2015/12/03/orthodox-rabbinic-statement-on-christianity/.

Common Courtesy Wikimedia. "German Protestant Church Denounces Anti-Semitism of Founder Martin Luther." The Forward. Accessed March 10, 2021. https://forward.com/news/breaking-news/324684/german-protestant-church-denounces-anti-semitism-of-founder-martin-luther/.

Danziger, Rachel Sharansky. "30 Years after Glienicke Bridge." Times of Israel, February 11, 2016. http://blogs.timesofisrael.com/30-years-after-glienicke-bridge/.

Desbois, Patrick, and Paul A Shapiro. *The Holocaust by bullets: a priest's journey to uncover the truth behind the murder of 1.5 million Jews.* Basingstoke: Palgrave Macmillan, 2010.

Edmunds, Donna R. "There Are 192,000 Holocaust Survivors Living in Israel - The Jerusalem Post." The Jerusalem Post | JPost.com. Accessed March 10, 2021. https://www.jpost.com/israel-news/there-are-192000-holocaust-survivors-living-in-israel-614407.

Eyzenbert, Eli Lizorkin. "Dr. Eli Lizorkin Eyzenberg - IIBS." Israel Institute of Biblical Studies. Accessed March 8, 2021. https://israelbiblicalstudies.com/teacher/eli-lizorkin-eyzenberg/.

Feavel, Doug. *A Storyteller's Anthology: 26 Inspiring Character Portraits For Our Time.* Abbotsford: Aneko Press, 2015.

Feldstein, Jonathan. "The Holocaust: Remember to Never Forget." Charisma News. Accessed September 19, 2021. https://www.charismanews.com/opinion/standing-with-israel/47234-the-holocaust-remember-to-never-forget.

Jewish Virtual Library. "Four Founders: - Mordecai Manuel Noah (1785–1851)." Accessed March 11, 2021. https://www.jewishvirtuallibrary.org/four-founders-emma-lazarus-judaic-treasures.

Freund, Michael. "Fundamentally Freund: Stop Calling It the 'Old Testament' - The Jerusalem Post." The Jerusalem Post | JPost.com, March 8, 2017. https://www.jpost.com/Opinion/Fundamentally-Freund-Stop-calling-it-the-Old-Testament-483640.

Israel Christian Nexus. "Gen. Shimon Erem Z"L," 2009. http://icnexus.org/gen-shimon-erem.

Gertz, Steven. "Opponents of Allegory." Christian History | Learn the History of Christianity & the Church. Accessed March 8, 2021. https://www.christianitytoday.com/history/issues/issue-80/opponents-of-allegory.html.

Griffin, Richard. *They Sang Louder*. Grace Point Publishing, 2013.

Gritsch, Eric W. "Was Luther Anti-Semitic." *Christian History*, 1993. https://christianhistoryinstitute.org/uploaded/50cf7fdbd09b24.47881377.pdf.

Religion Library - Roman Catholicism. "Historical Perspectives." Accessed March 8, 2021. https://www.patheos.com/library/roman-catholicism/origins/historical-perspectives.

Inbar, Efraim. "The Burden of the 1967 Victory." Begin-Sadat Center for Strategic Studies, April 5, 2017. https://besacenter.org/perspectives-papers/burden-1967-victory/.

"More U.S. Protestants Have No Specific Denominational Identity." Gallup, July 18, 2017. https://news.gallup.com/poll/214208/protestants-no-specific-denominational-identity.aspx.

"'Jews Are the Children of Satan' and the Dangers of Taking John 8:44 out of Context - CBS News," October 31, 2018. https://www.cbsnews.com/news/jews-are-the-children-of-satan-john-8-44-danger-of-taking-biblical-passages-out-of-context/.

Kertzer, David I. "What the Vatican's Secret Archives Are About to Reveal." The Atlantic, March 2, 2020. https://www.theatlantic.com/ideas/archive/2020/03/what-vaticans-secret-archives-are-about-reveal/607261/.

Lambert, Lance. *Battle for Israel*. Eastbourne, East Sussex:

Kingsway Publications, 1988.

Langer, Armen. "'Anti-Semitism' or 'Antisemitism'? And Why the Hyphen Matters." Evolve, October 29, 2018. http://evolve.reconstructingjudaism.org/antisemitism-hyphen.

Lapham, Steven. "Ten U.S. Churches Now Sanction Israel—To Some Degree, and with Caveats." WRMEA, March 2019. https://www.wrmea.org/2019-march-april/ten-us-churches-now-sanction-israel-to-some-degree-and-with-caveats.html.

Lizorkin-Eyzenberg, Eli. *The Jewish Apostle Paul: Rethinking One of the Greatest Jews That Ever Lived*. Edited by Ludmila Lizorkina, n.d.

Lockyer, Herbert. *All the Men of the Bible*. Grand Rapids: Zondervan, 2016. https://public.ebookcentral.proquest.com/choice/publicfullrecord.aspx?p=5397798.

———. *All the Women of the Bible*. Revised edition. Grand Rapids: Zondervan Academic, 1988.

Luther, Martin. *The Jews and Their Lies*. York, SC: Liberty Bell Publications, 2004.

Madden, Thomas. "Truth about the Spanish Inquisition." Catholic Culture. Accessed March 10, 2021. https://www.catholicculture.org/culture/library/view.cfm?id=5236&repos=1&subrepos=0&searchid=2097068.

Martin, Jason. "An Abandonment of Hope: Martin Luther and the Jews," n.d. https://www.biblicalstudies.org.uk/pdf/churchman/107-04_331.pdf.

McKim, Donald K., ed. *Historical Handbook of Major Biblical Interpreters*. 1st edition. Downers Grove: Intervarsity Pr, 1998.

"Medieval Inquisition." In *Wikipedia*, February 4, 2021. https://en.wikipedia.org/w/index.php?title=Medieval_Inquisition&oldid=1004831910.

Meir, Tamar. "Orpah: Midrash and Aggadah." Jewish Women's Archive. Accessed March 9, 2021. https://jwa.org/encyclopedia/article/orpah-midrash-and-aggadah.

Miller, Dr. Yvette Alt. "The Priest Uncovering Hidden Atrocities of the Holocaust." aish.com, November 7, 2015. https://www.aish.com/jw/s/The-Priest-Uncovering-Hidden-Atrocities-of-the-Holocaust.html.

Miller, Dr. Yvette Miller. "Aish Ha Torah." *The Priest Uncovering Hidden Atrocities of the Holocaust* (blog), November 7, 2015. https://www.aish.com/jw/s/The-Priest-Uncovering-Hidden-Atrocities-of-the-Holocaust.html?s=rab.

Miller, Emily McFarland, and Tom Heneghan. "The Nazis Exploited Martin Luther's Legacy." Sojourners, n.d. https://sojo.net/articles/nazis-exploited-martin-luther-s-legacy-berlin-exhibit-highlights-how.

Molotsky, Irvin. "Red Cross Admits Knowing of the Holocaust During the War." *The New York Times*, December 15, 1996, sec. U.S. https://www.nytimes.com/1996/12/19/us/red-cross-admits-knowing-of-the-holocaust-during-the-war.html.

Morse, Arthur D. *While Six Million Died; a Chronicle of American Apathy*. First Edition. Random House, 1968.

"New King James Version (NKJV) - Version Information - BibleGateway.Com." Accessed March 8, 2021. https://www.biblegateway.com/versions/New-King-James-Version-NKJV-Bible/.

Noah, M. M. *Discourse on the Restoration of the Jews: Delivered at the Tabernacle*, Oct. 28 and Dec. 2, 1844. Nineteenth Century Collections Online: Religion, Society, Spirituality, and Reform. New-York: Harper & Brothers, 1845.

Norwood, Stephen H. "Marauding Youth and the Christian Front: Antisemitic Violence in Boston and New York During World War II." *American Jewish History* 91, no. 2 (2003): 233–67. https://www.jstor.org/stable/23887201?seq=1.

Paras, Emily. "The Darker Side of Martin Luther." Accessed December 31, 2020. https://www.iwu.edu/history/constructingthepastvol9/Paras.pdf.

Parsons, John. "Should Christians Celebrate Purim." Hebrews for Christians, February 2010. https://hebrew4christians.com/About_HFC/Site_News/Archive-2010/February/february.html.

Pfann, Claire. "Who Is My Brother." Accessed September 21, 2021. https://jcstudies.store/who-is-my-brother-vital-lessons-from-the-acts-of-the-apostles/.

Philpot, Robert. "Church of England Report Admits Christians Anti-Semitism Helped Lead to Holocaust." *The Times of Israel*. November 22, 2019, online edition. https://www.timesofisrael.com/church-of-england-report-admits-christian-anti-semitism-led-to-holocaust/.

Pink, Arthur W. "Jesus Laid Down His Life?" Christianity. com, September 20, 2010. https://www.christianity.com/jesus/death-and-resurrection/the-crucifixion/jesus-laid-down-his-life.html.

———. *Seven Sayings of the Saviour on the Cross*. Grand Rapids: Baker Books, 2007.

Prince, Derek. *Blessing or Curse: You Can Choose*. Grand Rapids: Chosen Books, 1990.

———. *Our Debt to Israel*. DPM-UK 2014. Baldock, UK: DPM-UK, 2015.

Yad Vashem. "Protestant Pastor Andre Trocme | Under the Wings of the Church | Themes | A Tribute to the Righteous Among the Nations." Accessed March 2, 2021. https://www.yadvashem.org/yv/en/exhibitions/righteous/trocme.asp.

Ravenhill, Leonard. *Why Revival Tarries*. 2007 edition. Minneapolis, Minn: Bethany House Publishers, 2004.

Jewish Virtual Library. "Refusniks." Accessed March 7, 2021. https://www.jewishvirtuallibrary.org/refusniks.

Ritmeyer, Author Leen. "Bethlehem – the Manger and the

Inn." Ritmeyer Archaeological Design (blog), December 14, 2014. https://www.ritmeyer.com/2014/12/14/bethlehem-the-inn-and-the-manger/.

Rosenfeld, Rabbi David. "Jethro's Many Names: Ask the Rabbi Response." Ask The Rabbi. Accessed March 9, 2021. https://www.aish.com/atr/Jethro-Many-Names.html.

Ross, Robert W. *So It Was True : The American Protestant Press and the Nazi Persecution of the Jews*. First Edition. Minneapolis: University of Minnesota Press, 1980.

Roth, John K., Elisabeth Maxwell, Margot Levy, and Wendy Whitworth, eds. *Remembering for the Future: The Holocaust in an Age of Genocide*. London: Palgrave Macmillan UK, 2001. https://doi.org/10.1007/978-1-349-66019-3.

Sales, Ben. "Archaeologist Believes He's Found Site of Jesus's Trial by Pontius Pilate," April 6, 2015. http://www.timesofisrael.com/archaeologist-believes-hes-found-site-of-jesuss-trial-by-pontius-pilate.

Sanders, Sharon. "A Place for My People." *For Zion's Sake*, 2016.

———. "Teaching on Israel and the Church," n.d., 8.

Schechter, Solomon, Emil G. Hirsch, and Eduard Konig. "Elisha." In *Jewish Encyclopedia*, December 21, 2020. http://www.jewishencyclopedia.com/articles/5682-elisha.

"SHEMOT – Edmond J. Safra's Synagogue." Accessed March 2, 2021. http://www.sinagogadeipanema.com.br/en/

sermon/shemot/.

"The Seven Sayings of the Saviour on the Cross." Accessed
March 8, 2021. https://chapellibrary.org:8443/pdf/
books/ssot.pdf.

Stanley, Alessandra. "Pope Asks Forgiveness for Errors Of the
Church Over 2,000 Years." *The New York Times*, March 13,
2000, sec. World. https://www.nytimes.com/2000/03/13/
world/pope-asks-forgiveness-for-errors-of-the-church-
over-2000-years.html.

U.S. Embassy in Israel. "Statement by Former President Trump
on Jerusalem," December 7, 2020. http://il.usembassy.gov/
statement-by-president-trump-on-jerusalem/.

Tenoria, Rich. "Jesuit Catholic Priest Pens Book about His
Order's Complicity in the Holocaust | The Times of
Israel." The Times of Israel, November 10, 2020. https://
www.timesofisrael.com/jesuit-catholic-priest-pens-book-
about-his-orders-complicity-in-the-holocaust/.

Jewish Virtual Library. "The Inquisition." Accessed March
10, 2021. https://www.jewishvirtuallibrary.org/the-
inquisition.

"The Opposite of Love Is Not Hate, But Indifference – Quote
Investigator," May 21, 2019. https://quoteinvestigator.
com/2019/05/21/indifference/.

"The Pope, the Jews, and the Secrets in the Archives - The
Atlantic." Accessed March 3, 2021. https://www.
theatlantic.com/ideas/archive/2020/08/the-popes-

jews/615736/.

Begin-Sadat Center for Strategic Studies. "The Social Geography of the BDS Movement and Antisemitism," August 8, 2019. https://besacenter.org/perspectives-papers/social-geography-bds-antisemitism/.

Israel Ministry of Foreign Affairs. "The State of Israel Is Born." Accessed March 14, 2021. https://mfa.gov.il/mfa/aboutisrael/israelat50/pages/the%20state%20of%20israel%20is%20born.aspx.

Thomson, J.R. "An Incorruptible Crown." Electronic Database. The Pulpit Commentary. Accessed March 12, 2021. https://biblehub.com/sermons/auth/thomson/an_incorruptible_crown.htm.

Sinagoga Edmod J. Safra. "Turning Curses into Blessings," December 28, 2015. http://www.sinagogadeipanema.com.br/en/sermon/shemot/.

United States Holocaust Memorial Museum, Washington, DC. "Le Chambon-Sur-Lignon." Holocaust Encyclopedia. Accessed March 12, 2021. https://encyclopedia.ushmm.org/content/en/article/le-chambon-sur-lignon.

Wiles, Jeremy. *Sing a Little Louder*. Holland: KingdomWorks Studios. Accessed March 8, 2021. https://kingdomworks.com/films/sing-a-little-louder/?ims=cw-102416.

Jewish Virtual Library. "Wilhelm Marr - League of Antisemites." Accessed March 5, 2021. https://www.jewishvirtuallibrary.org/wilhelm-marr.

Wilson, Stephen Douglas. "Where Was Jesus Tried?" Baptist Press. April 1, 2015. https://www.baptistpress.com/resource-library/news/where-was-jesus-tried.

Wolicki, Pesach. "A New Christian Antisemitism - The Jerusalem Post." The Jerusalem Post | JPost.com, November 28, 2019. https://www.jpost.com/opinion/a-new-christian-antisemitism-609334.

Young, Brad H. *The Hebrew Heritage Bible Newer Testament.* Tulsa: Hebrew Heritage Bible society, 2020.

About the Author

Sharon Sanders is cofounder of Christian Friends of Israel, Jerusalem (CFI) with her husband, Ray Sanders. As a result of Parkinson's, Ray is now the executive director/international director, emeritus. Sharon still works with enthusiasm for the nation of Israel and is currently interim executive director.

Established in December 1985, CFI's founding member nations consisted of the United Kingdom, the United States, and France. The pro-Israel Christian ministry is international in scope, with its headquarters in Jerusalem and recognized representatives worldwide.

Sharon received her early Christian education in the Methodist Church in Hartsburg, Illinois (USA). She also was a delegate to Wesleyan University summer school. Later in life, she was a part of Lutheran, and subsequently, Pentecostal and Charismatic circles.

One of her teenage years' most memorable events was being selected for a group of outstanding young musicians across the United States to represent America to Europe. As a charter member of the School Band and Chorus of America, an impressive group of aspiring young musicians, she toured Europe with a distinguished open air-marching and concert hall music band and performed in the concert choir. She became a charter member of the SBCA, in cooperation with the United States Government-sponsored People to People Program, under the direction of Edward R. Murrow, a prominent American broadcast journalist during the years of 1963 and 1964. She also attended the University of Illinois, Champaign-Urbana, music school.

Later, she studied business law in Peoria, Illinois, while working as a legal secretary for a private law firm. In her pursuit to be a paralegal, she was employed by the Illinois Supreme Court Reporters Office and served as an assistant to a circuit court judge in a Law and Justice Center in Bloomington, Illinois. Career directions changed when God transformed both Ray and Sharon Sander's lives.

Ray and Sharon were born again and spirit-filled during a powerful move of the Holy Spirit in 1975 in Bloomington, Illinois, USA. Along with her husband Ray and daughter Stacey Beth, she was baptized in the Assembly of God church, in Normal, Illinois, in the 1970s. In the late '70s, as a family, they attended a systematic Bible study congregation at the Good News Teaching Center, Champaign-Urbana, Illinois.

In 1983, Ray and Sharon left their professional business careers. They enrolled full-time at Christ for the Nations, Dallas, Texas, an interdenominational Bible college (www. cfni.org). There they both graduated and received ministerial ordinations. Sharon was personally ordained by Dr. Freda Lindsay, cofounder and president of CFNI. Stacey married the same year, in which Ray and Sharon enrolled at CFNI. Subsequently, after following their own professional business careers, Stacey and her husband, Kevin, graduated from CFNI in Dallas and became ordained ministers. Honoring the thirty-year legacy of Stacey's parents in Jerusalem and a family heritage of six generations of believers, the Howards received the mantle of leadership from 2015–2019.

Throughout the years, since Ray and Sharon's arrival in Israel, in June 1985 and the ultimate establishment of CFI, in December 1985, both Ray and Sharon studied Christianity's Jewish heritage. They learned about Israel and the church under the systematic teachings of Dr. Derek Prince (Eaton College/ Kings College, Cambridge) and Reverend Lance Lambert (London University). For nearly twenty years, Sharon expanded her understanding through these "fathers of the faith" and Bible teachers such as Johannes Facius of Germany and Dwight Pryor of the United States.

Added to these periods of learning, she spent eighteen incredible and fantastic years in private discussions with an Orthodox rabbi, Yaakov Youlis, a descendant of Avram Shag, the former chief rabbi of Hungary. This rare opportunity was given to her, which was most often denied to non-Jews, especially women. Rabbi Yaacov offered many insights from a Hebrew mindset and training in the Hebraic context of the Bible during the studies they shared until his passing on 30 May 2011.

Numerous generals of the Christian faith have endorsed and sanctioned the work of Christian Friends of Israel, including the late Dr. Freda Lindsay (CFNI), Dr. Derek Prince (Derek Prince Ministries), and the late Reverend Lance Lambert, Dr. Delmar Guines, former president of South Western University (Dallas, Texas), Dr. Ray Gannon, Assemblies of God (MJBI VP for Academic Affairs), Dr. Jeff Seif (University Distinguished Professor of Bible and Jewish Studies) as well as Pastor Wayne Hilsden (Canadian Assemblies of God and former Senior Pastor at King of Kings Community, Jerusalem), and Peter Kent (former president of the International Chamber of Commerce Redwood, California) to name a few distinguished figures who stood shoulder to shoulder with the Sanders and Christian Friends of Israel throughout their ministry years.

Sharon's strengths are in Christian–Jewish education; having studied Jewish–Christian relations through Hebrew University, she is an avid reader of scholarly literature on the subject. As a Christian, she has been privileged to live in Israel among the Jewish people for over thirty years. She and Ray established CFI as a legally registered, pioneer pro-Israel, Christian Zionist ministry. Her grassroots experiences continue to take her beneath the soil into intimate and personal Jewish life. Her stories and testimonies touch the hearts of people around the world as she shares the long and winding, adventurous road on which few Christians have traveled.

During their tenure in Israel, Sharon and Ray spoke in fifty nations abroad, teaching about Israel and the Jewish people and CFI. In conferences and meeting halls everywhere, the Sanders were always warmly received. Having acquired an expanded view of how Jews and Christians "*think*" positioned her to assist both faith communities in relating to one another in the ongoing development of Jewish–Christians relations.

Sharon's vision for the future is to be a blessing to Israel and the church. Derek Prince's understanding of retirement was, "show it to me in the Bible, and I will do it!" She utilizes her years of experience through speaking, teaching, writing, meeting with tour groups to Israel, and community involvement in Jerusalem. She enjoys speaking to Israeli audiences as well as Christian assemblies.

The years of life and service in Israel have been some of the hardest for the Sanders, but the very best. They were granted permanent residency in Israel (in 2004), where they plan to reside the rest of their lives.

CPSIA information can be obtained
at www.ICGtesting.com
Printed in the USA
BVHW070441291122
653004BV00001B/3